Composting

The Ultimate Guide to Creating Your Own Organic Compost in Your Backyard and Using It for Organic Gardening to Create a More Self-Sufficient Garden

Contents

INTRODUCTION 1

CHAPTER ONE: INTRODUCTION TO ORGANIC COMPOSTING 3

    UNDERSTAND THE SCIENCE BEHIND COMPOSTING 10

CHAPTER TWO: CHOOSING THE BEST TOOLS 15

    COMPOSTING BIN 15

    HOW TO BUILD A BASIC DIY COMPOST BIN 26

    BUILD A THREE-CRATE BIN SYSTEM 28

CHAPTER THREE: BUILD YOUR ORGANIC COMPOST PILE 32

    COMPOST MATERIALS 39

    COMPOSTING METHODS 43

    STEPS TO BUILDING A COMPOST PILE 45

    TURNING AND AERATING YOUR COMPOST PILE 47

CHAPTER FOUR: SPEEDING UP THE PROCESS WITH ORGANIC
ACTIVATORS 50

    NATURAL ACTIVATORS 52

    MICROBES AND ENZYME ACTIVATORS 53

    HOW TO GET DIY COMPOST ACTIVATORS 55

CHAPTER FIVE: HOT OR COLD COMPOSTING 57

Hot Composting 58

Cold Composting.. 62

Warm Composting 67

CHAPTER SIX: VERMICOMPOSTING 69

Feeding the Worms 72

Kitchen Vermiculture 74

Making a Worm Tube.. 75

Harvesting Worms... 76

Vermicompost Tea 77

CHAPTER SEVEN: WORKING WITH CONTAINERS 79

How to Store Scraps for Your Compost Container...................... 84

CHAPTER EIGHT: WORKING WITHOUT CONTAINERS 87

Trench Composting 89

CHAPTER NINE: KEEPING PESTS OUT....................................92

How to Protect Your Compost from Rats and Mice........................ 94

How to Get Rid of Raccoons 97

Predator Urine as a Pest Deterrent 99

CHAPTER TEN: TIPS ON HOW TO BEST USE YOUR COMPOST........101

How to Store Compost... 108

CHAPTER ELEVEN: COMPOST MAINTENANCE TIPS 110

How to Know if Your Compost Pile Is Struggling 113

CHAPTER TWELVE: GROWING PLANTS FOR A COMPOST PILE.......115

CONCLUSION...118

HERE'S ANOTHER BOOK BY DION ROSSER THAT YOU MIGHT
LIKE 119

REFERENCES 120

Introduction

Organic composting. These two words sound like they involve sizeable industrial equipment and vast agricultural space. Chances are you've never thought of making your own organic compost, and most people think it is reserved for farmers and large agricultural companies.

In reality, organic composting is the practice of making valuable soil humus from decomposing materials. Based on this definition, you can already tell this is something you should have no problem setting up in your home.

For years, humans have been using compost to improve soil structure and quality to facilitate better and healthier plant growth. In the past, we had to purchase compost from agricultural stores nearby, but in recent years, gardeners have taken the initiative to start making their very own organic compost at home.

This book provides in-depth information on organic composting in a home garden. From beginning to end, you will find valuable information on how to start making organic compost from the scraps in your kitchen and the dry materials all around you.

Anything is compostable, as long as you know which methods to implement and how you will apply them. Luckily, this is where this book comes in. In *Organic Composting*, you will learn what composting entails, the different methods, and the best techniques to create quality organic compost.

The first chapter introduces you to organic composting and the science behind it. How do organic materials turn into fine soil for plants? Who or what makes that happen? What are the stages involved in the process? Those are some of the questions that are answered in the beginning.

Once you have understood the basics of composting, it's time to get your hands dirty and implement the knowledge you have learned. From finding the best composting tools to the optimal material for producing rich compost!

Organic composting is for anyone looking to learn how to use compost to improve the quality of their yields – or who just wants to do their part for the environment. It does not matter whether you are a beginner or an experienced gardener. There is something for everyone in the book.

Ready to dive into the intriguing world of organic composting? Start reading to begin your journey!

Chapter One: Introduction to Organic Composting

Composting is simple. It is the process of naturally recycling organic matter (food scraps, leaves, etc.) into a nutrient-filled fertilizer to enrich your soil and, subsequently, your plants. A simple way to put it would be, compost can be defined as "decayed organic matter."

Everything that grows in a horticultural environment decomposes after a while. When done right, composting provides a suitable environment for fungi, bacteria, nematodes, worms, sowbugs, and other organisms to hasten the decomposing process without the intervention of chemical or artificial products.

Organic matter can refer to a wide range of things, from the twigs in your backyard to banana or orange peels. When you create a compost pile made out of these organic byproducts, they start breaking down naturally. The resulting matter from this process is called compost.

It typically looks like garden soil but is much more fertile. Organic compost is often called "black gold" by gardeners, growers, and farmers. It is richer in nutrients than ordinary gardening soil, and you can use it for all kinds of things, from simple gardening to industrial agriculture and horticulture.

Contrary to what you may have been led to believe, composting isn't as tricky or foul-smelling as people say. You can compost anywhere as long as you know and understand the fundamentals of the process.

You can compost almost everything, as long as it comes from the ground. Vegetable and fruit scraps such as carrot peels, avocado pits, pumpkin leftovers, cucumber ends can all go into a compost pile. Since grain also grows in the soil, you can add cereal, pasta, stale bread, and other items into a compost heap, as well. Basically, instead of throwing away scraps of uneaten foods into the trash, you'll just repurpose them.

Other things such as tea leaves, spices, coffee grounds, herbs, eggshells, and nuts are also suitable for making organic compost. You can also include disease-free plant trimmings and cut flowers. However, as much as there are things you can add to your compost heap, there are hundreds of things that you should definitely exclude.

Animal products, in general, are not acceptable in compost heaps. You cannot add fish, meat, butter, cheese, yogurt, animal fat, or milk. A general rule of thumb is to exclude anything greasy or oily from a compost pile.

Many people believe they can add their pets' poops to their compost because it is also organic. As logical as this may seem, it is not advisable. Your pet's poops can introduce certain diseases into the compost, which may render the pile unusable and end up being a waste of your time and resources.

You may already be familiar with composting since it is a widespread practice in many homes. But the term "organic composting" confuses a lot of people. If compost is already called "decayed organic matter," then what is organic compost?

Like most people, you probably have a vague idea of what the term "organic" means or encompasses. However, if you were asked to break down the specific definition, that might be a little easier said than done.

Nutritionally, "organic" describes anything that encompasses sustainability, environmental awareness, health consciousness, and is free of chemicals. But these words don't drill down on the true meaning of organic.

It is impossible to give a single, straightforward answer, but some vital definitions can help you understand what "organic" means.

First, you have "chemically organic," which means that the item contains the element carbon. For those who need a quick refresher, carbon is life's building block, and that is why all living things are called "carbon-based life forms." So, when you see a bag of soil marked as "rich in organics," it likely means carbon and living organisms are abundant.

Next, you have "agriculturally organic," which refers to produce grown naturally without using artificial chemicals. Today, it is a generic term for most produce you find in the grocery store with an "organic" label. Organic produce and plants are devoid of fertilizers, pesticides, fungicides, and herbicides. Livestock and their byproducts may also be described as organic as long as they are raised free of steroids, antibiotics, and hormones.

Lastly, there is produce that isn't labeled "organic" but is nonetheless organic. Some low-scale farmers and producers supply exclusively to farmers' markets and local grocery stores without USDA certification.

Now, when we talk about organic compost, it is essentially the same as regular compost. The critical difference is that the latter contains chemically organic compounds decomposed down to their most essential and valuable nutrients.

Finished organic compost contains nitrogen, a nutrient that is vital for both plants and animals. Nitrogen is found in enzymes, proteins, DNA, and other cellular structures. During the decomposition process, the decomposing organisms such as bacteria and fungi break down the nitrogen-based compounds in a compost heap into ammonium. Then, the bacteria in the soil turn the ammonium into nitrite, which then metamorphoses into nitrate. In the final phase, the nitrate metamorphoses into nitrogen, meaning that the organic compost is finally ready for use in your garden or farm.

For compost to become usable, it must go through all the phases mentioned above. Under-aged and poorly managed compost usually doesn't make it through the four stages. They often end up producing excessive ammonium in the soil with insufficient bacteria to jumpstart the nitrification process. In many cases, excessive unconverted ammonium can result in imbalanced, unusable, and counterproductive compost accompanied by a powerful, foul odor.

When you properly make and manage your compost, it can make your soil biologically and structurally diverse. If the decomposing organisms and microbes do their jobs as they should, well-made compost should have lots of little air pockets and a crumbly texture.

These tiny pockets and spaces can absorb and hold sufficient water, making a healthy compost heap perfect for retaining moisture. The high quality also means the soil will stick together, making it erosion-resistant. With proper aeration, a healthy compost heap can also host a wide range of microfauna to enhance your soil's biological diversity and speed up the decomposition process.

As you may already know, there are different bacteria and fungi species, and each species has a different niche. Some kick-start the first phase of decomposition, while others transform the nutrients into usable forms for plants. Some help manage the population of microbes.

When it comes to organic composting, diversity is highly essential. The more variety in your compost, the higher the quality will be. Compost is much more than ordinary "plant food." It is crucial to improving the health and productivity of your soil.

One question many people often ask is, "If the compost has everything soil and plants need, what differentiates it from fertilizer?" The critical difference between compost and fertilizer is how they both provide nutrients to soil and plants.

Compared to compost, fertilizer is purely a collection of nutrients, and its structure isn't as diverse and complex. In a way, it is also more potent because it instantaneously floods soil and plants with nutrients instead of steadily streaming it to them as compost does.

Organic compost reduces your need for fertilizer. Depending on your soil's pre-composting condition and the plants you grow, creating your personalized compost can effectively erase the need for fertilizer. This can help you achieve a healthier environment for your plants and the different ecosystems in your garden.

There are many reasons why you should consider organic composting in your home garden. The pros far outweigh the cons, if there are any.

First, composting offers an excellent way to recycle all the organic waste generated in your home. Statistics show that garden waste and food scraps make up over 28% of the things we get rid of.

Not only do food scraps significantly burden the environment, but their processing is also quite expensive. In the United States, landfilling municipal solid waste costs up to $55 per ton in 2020. Making your organic compost at home is an effective way of diverting solid waste from landfills and turning it into something that can benefit your garden and yard.

Usually, the organic matter goes through aerobic decomposition when it's broken down; put another way, most of the job is performed by microorganisms that need oxygen. In a landfill, however, compostable waste is buried along with vast amounts of trash. This can cut off the oxygen supply for the decomposing microorganisms.

Instead of aerobic decomposition, the waste goes through anaerobic decomposition instead – meaning that it is broken down by microorganisms that don't require free-flowing oxygen to live or survive. The result of that is the production of biogas, which is usually 50% carbon dioxide and 50% methane.

Both methane and carbon dioxide are potent greenhouse gases, meaning they can harm the surrounding environment and trap heat in the atmosphere for many years. A typical modern landfill is built with a methane capture system to prevent this, but the procedure usually doesn't get a hold of all the gas.

Composting within the comfort of your home can significantly reduce methane emissions from landfills. Landfills are a significant source of man-generated methane emissions in the U.S. However, since the United States' solid waste system is built around landfilling, just 6 percent of waste gets composted.

You can do your part in changing this by increasing the composting and recycling rates to reduce the waste generation in your home. This, in turn, will reduce the harmful gases to our atmosphere and the ozone layer.

Another reason to try organic composting is to help improve soil health and reduce erosion, especially if you have a large-scale agricultural system or a garden. Organic compost contains nitrogen, phosphorus, and potassium—three essential nutrients that garden crops need an abundance of to thrive. Additionally, organic compost also has other useful nutrients such as calcium, iron, zinc, and magnesium.

Instead of using synthetic fertilizers containing dangerous chemicals that can affect your soil and plants' quality and health, composting offers an organic alternative. Agricultural research on the effects of soil health and crop productivity has established that compost can retain water and improve plant productivity and resilience.

Agriculture accounts for around 80 percent of the United States' water use. As a farmer, you most likely have an irrigation system in place. Those systems can be expensive to set up and operate despite their efficiency.

You may not know that the soil's water-remaining capacities increase when you add organic matter to the mixture. The addition of only 1 percent of organic matter to the soil makes it capable of holding up to 20 thousand gallons of water per acre.

Through organic composting, you can foster your soil's health and effectively reduce your water usage without worrying about crop yields. Compared to using non-composted soil, you will have higher yields.

You can do composting both inside and outside your home. Depending on what you want or hope to achieve, the process can be straightforward or complicated. There are different types of compost you can create for your home garden. But it is important to know that certain factors will determine which methods you can use. These factors include:

- Space availability
- Amount of available organic waste
- Type of organic waste (yard or kitchen waste)
- Amount of time devoted to the composting process

In a subsequent chapter, you will find out more about the two types of composting and which one to choose for your home garden, depending on the above factors.

Understand the Science Behind Composting

Earlier, you learned that microorganisms are crucial to composting and are everywhere around you. You also learned that the key to effective organic composting is to create the ideal environment for those microorganisms to thrive–moisture, warmth, nutrients, and sufficient oxygen.

Different phases make up the composting process, and various microorganisms are involved in each of these phases. Below is a breakdown of each stage and the ideal temperature, moisture, oxygen, and nutrients needed to produce a healthy compost heap.

The first stage of composting only lasts a few days, during which mesophilic microorganisms that thrive between 68 - 113°F begin to break down the organic matter physically in a compost heap. This stage naturally leads to heat production, causing the temperature to rise to over 105 degrees.

Once temperatures hit 105°F, thermophilic microorganisms, or bacteria that thrive in higher temperatures, will replace the mesophilic microorganisms in the second composting stage. This can last between a few days and several months.

The thermophilic microbes further break down the organic matter, and your compost heap should begin to turn a dark shade of brown. The higher temperature allows them to break down complex carbohydrates, protein, and fat into more refined pieces. During the second stage, the temperature continues to increase.

Without care, the pile can become so hot that the decomposing microbes eventually die off. To avoid this, you need to aerate and turn over the compost heap regularly. That will keep the temperature below 145 degrees and provide complimentary oxygen to the microorganisms within the compost.

The final stage lasts for several months. It starts when the microbes use up the available compounds supply, after which temperature starts dropping enough for mesophilic microbes to take over the decomposition process once again. Subsequently, they will break down the remaining organic matter into usable compost for your soil and plants.

As explained earlier, aerobes and anaerobes are the two categories of decomposing microbes you'll find in a compost pile. Aerobes are essential microbes for composting. They require a minimum of a 5 percent oxygen level to survive in the compost. They consume and absorb the organic waste in the compost pile and excrete nitrogen, phosphorus, and magnesium – the essential nutrients plants need to grow healthily.

In contrast, anaerobes don't require oxygen to survive. They also aren't nearly as efficient at decomposing as aerobes. Most anaerobes also emit chemicals that may be toxic to your plants. They can affect the smell of your compost pile by releasing hydrogen sulfide, which makes it smell like rotten eggs.

Usually, a compost pile contains 80 to 90 percent of bacteria, while the remaining 10 to 20 percent are fungi species such as yeasts and mold. Additionally, suppose you create the right environment and condition. In that case, more helpful garden fauna such as worms, centipedes, and pill bugs will sneak into the compost pile and help break down the organic waste until it turns into nutrient-rich soil.

The United States Environmental Protection Agency (EPA) suggests that you need a mix of "greens" and "browns" to create the ideal composting environment. "Greens" refer to nitrogen-rich organic items such as fruits and veggies waste, grass clippings, and coffee grounds. "Browns" are carbon-rich items such as dead leaves, twigs, branches, and other tree or plant clippings.

Rapid composting is achievable with a 25:1 to 30:1 carbon-to-nitrogen ratio. Microbes consume both carbon and nitrogen for energy and additional nutrition, respectively.

When a compost pile contains too much carbon, it generates less heat due to the inability of the microbes to grow and reproduce readily and break down carbon effectively. The result of this is a slower decomposition rate. On the other hand, an excess of nitrogen increases the acidity of the heap. This leads to a strong, off-putting ammonia smell that can be toxic for some useful microbe species in your composting pile.

Adequate moisture is also key to the health of the decomposing microorganisms in a composting pile. You need a 40 to 60 percent moisture content to achieve sufficient dampness to keep the organisms alive and thriving without forcing the oxygen out of the heap.

Keep in mind that the amount of oxygen in a compost heap is just as crucial since an oxygen deficit would allow anaerobes to take charge of the pile. You already know what the by-product of that will be.

Again, you can increase oxygen levels by turning over and stirring the pile.

Below is a more comprehensive list of items you can compost:

- Eggshells
- Fruits
- Vegetables
- Nutshells
- Shredded paper, newspaper, and cardboard
- Teabags
- Coffee grounds and filters
- Houseplants
- Grass, leaves, twigs, branches, and other yard trimmings
- Sawdust
- Hay and straw
- Cotton
- Wool rugs
- Woodchips
- Hair and fur
- Lint from the dryer and vacuum cleaner
- Ashes from the fireplace

What not to compost:

- Leaves and twigs from specific trees like Black Walnut that release potentially toxic substances. (Before adding brown material, make sure you know what type of plant or tree it originated from)
- Dairy products, including fish or meat scraps and bones, eggs, fats, oils, etc. These can cause possible odor problems by attracting pests such as houseflies and rodents.

• Coal and coal ash because they contain substances that are toxic for your plants

• Diseased or infected houseplants as they may pass on the disease to other plants

• Chemically treated yard trimmings with the potential to kill your composting microbes

• Waste from your cat or dog, as this might be potentially harmful due to bacteria, parasites, and viruses

Note that you should only add dairy products to your composting pile if you think that you can effectively deal with the smell and the various pathogens present in them.

Many other items and products are being developed for eventual inclusion in composting piles. Some of these include garbage bags, dinnerware, flatware, and even diapers. But you must ensure that these products are safe for home composting before you add them to your pile.

This chapter was just an overview and introduction to organic composting. In the next set of chapters, we will delve deeper into the process and how you can build your very own stench-free composting pile.

The next chapter explicitly covers the tools you need to create organic compost within the comfort of your home. Read on to find out!

Chapter Two: Choosing the Best Tools

You cannot start composting without the proper tools. Some tools are essential in building your compost pile, while others help with maintenance. In this chapter, you will find out which tools you need to start making your own compost.

As a gardener, you most likely own most of the tools needed for composting already. In every aspect of gardening, having the proper tools for a task is crucial because it makes the job easier. Here are the best tools required for basic composting activities.

Composting Bin

A composting bin or container is necessary if you live in an apartment without backyard space to build a compost pile. It also helps if you have concerns about attracting rodents into your home due to the food scraps.

Usually, the kind of composting bin you get will depend on whether you plan to turn your compost manually or automatically. Certain composters can get the job done all by themselves. You can also build a DIY bin.

To make the process of choosing the right compost bin easier for you, below are some commonly used bins amongst composters and farmers:

  • **Basic Composter:** This is a self-contained bin with a lid to keep the compost covered and out of the reach of pets or other wildlife. It is the perfect choice for urban gardeners and those with small yards.

  • **Indoor Composter:** This is for those without the outdoor space for composting. This small kitchen composter works without electricity and can be kept under the sink or cabinets. You can create compost in as little as two weeks with this handy unit.

  • **Spinning Composter:** A spinning composting unit helps to keep the pile aerated with a single turn of the handle. Although more expensive than basic composting bins, it can help make compost in no time.

  • **Worm Composter:** This is used in vermicomposting practices. The units are self-contained. It may take a while to understand how to operate them. But once you figure them out, there is no limit to the amount of compost you can make.

  • **Electric Composter:** If your budget is slightly stretchable, an electric composter is just the right one for you. Used for hot composting, this modern unit fits in a kitchen with its compact size and look. You can store up to 5 pounds of food per day in the electric composter. In two weeks, you should have sufficient nitrogen-rich compost to mix in with your soil. Unlike the other composter, you can add everything, including meat, bones, and other dairy products, into an electric composter.

• **Homemade Bin:** You can make a compost bin from just about any material, from scrap lumber to old wooden pallets, chicken wire, and even cinder blocks. If you have large drums, you may even be able to make your own spinning composter. A homemade bin requires some hard, manual work but is less expensive than retail composters in the long run.

The perfect compost bin fits your available space, matches your budget range, and does the job you want it to do.

The compost bin should be ready before you start building the pile. If you live in a home with enough backyard space, you can construct your pile directly into the ground.

There are two home versions of composting bins. The first is called the Log Cabin – an easy-to-build system that consists of 4 x 4 planks of wood arranged on top of each other like logs in a cabin. Their ends don't fit, and the sides remain comparatively open to ensure good airflow.

In a log cabin composter, you need to remove the bottom plank whenever it's time to collect some compost. Then, you'll push in some bricks at the ends in place of the board to create support for the other boards. That leaves sufficient space for you to scoop out your finished compost when you need to.

Another type of composting bin is the Chicken-Wire Bin which consists of round, square, hexagonal, etc. containers. The bins can be of almost any shape. Some have wooden frames, while others simply have a mast or two to hold the structure in place. These bins are built light so that you can simply lift the bin, set it down, and use a fork to turn the pile during turning time.

You will learn more in-depth instructions on how to build your basic composting bin further down the line. If you don't want to make your DIY bin, you can purchase a standard composter from your local store. Also called a compost digester, this typically consists of enclosed sides and top. It opens at the bottom, meaning you can set it directly on the ground in your backyard. This composter is common in residential areas where homes have smaller bins enclosed enough to keep pests out.

Standard composting bins are inexpensive, but they aren't recommended to produce organic compost within a specific timeframe. Compost is typically challenging to turn in digesters, so it might take several months to make usable compost.

The final option is composting in a tumbler. For good reasons, this is considered the most efficient composting bin. The whole process is automatic because tumblers are designed to aerate and turn the compost automatically. However, it is also quite expensive. So, if you are working with a budget, you should consider building your bin and doing all the work manually.

Kitchen Pail or Crock

A kitchen pail or crock is essential for collecting food and table scraps from coffee grounds to potato and onion peels. Using a pail reduces the number of trips you have to make from your kitchen to your compost pin.

Pails and crocks come in varying materials, including plastic, stainless steel, bamboo, and ceramic. Some materials are more expensive than others. Choose a kitchen pail material that is within your budget and suitable for your environment.

Ensure the container you get has a lid to prevent the compost odor from infiltrating or permeating your kitchen. Another way to prevent odor is to line the inside of the pail with compostable plastic. This makes it easier to move the solid waste to your composting bin whenever you need to add more material.

Fork or Hand Cultivator

You need a fork or hand cultivator to add scraps and waste to your compost heap without touching the bin. Forks have four to five long, thin, and upward-curving tines meant to help you scoop the organic matter to the compost pile location.

They are especially effective for moving huge chumps of bulky organic items such as leaves plant trimmings, hay, and straw. You can also use them to build new piles and turn them until all the organic waste is sufficiently decomposed.

Another tool you should consider getting is a soil fork for turning almost-ready compost and digging up finished compost from the heap so you can mix it into your garden beds or planting containers.

Shovel and Spade

A shovel is generally designed for moving material from one location to another without it falling off. The raised lips on both sides of the shovels stop bits of the material from falling off. On the other hand, a spade is effective for digging thanks to its straight, sharp head.

Both shovel and spade are designed in different styles with minor variations to improve their suitability for specific gardening tasks. A round-bladed shovel is an all-purpose tool that you can use for turning almost-ready compost, scooping finished compost from the pile, mixing compost into your soil, and digging holes in loamy, sandy, and loose soils.

If you need something a little more versatile, a pointed-blade shovel is a good choice. It does everything the round-bladed shovel does while allowing you to dig more easily into compacted soil. You can also use the pointed blade to chop up organic waste into smaller pieces before adding it to the compost pile.

Quality Hose

You need to keep things adequately moist in your composting bin. Therefore, it is essential to have easy access to water. Don't forget that moisture is one of the most critical components of successful organic composting.

Of course, you can get a cheap, low-quality hose if you want, but it's much better to get a high-quality hose because the cheap ones always have a host of problems, from kinking to cracking or refusing to coil. If you don't get a quality hose from the start, you'll eventually have to purchase another one.

Spend money on a high-quality hose for adding water to your compost pile. It is recommended to add a nozzle to the hose to turn the water flow on and off with minimal effort and control the amount of water you add into your pile. Overwatering can reverse your hard work.

Turner or Aerator

A compost turner allows you to add essential oxygen to your pile so that the microbes can stay active and continue to thrive. You can purchase a specially made turner from a physical or online store. Most have pointed ends that you can stab into the compost heap and wings that make large air pockets deep within the pile.

With an aerator, you don't need to worry about turning your pile more frequently than required. An aerator is designed to penetrate dense matter comfortably. When you stick one into your heap and pull it back up, don't be surprised that waste at the bottom of the heap will come to the surface.

There are two types of aerators you can purchase for composting: screw aerators and wing aerators.

Screw aerators have a large screw attached to the handle or an electric drill, depending on which you choose. Most of the screws look pretty delicate, while others are hefty. If the aerator has a corkscrew design, that means it can penetrate deep into the compost pile without you putting in too much effort.

A screw aerator will pull up buried materials when you stop turning and pull them out of the pile. You can easily make one with a stick and screw auger.

Winged aerators are designed with a three-to-four-foot-long metal rod to serve as a handle and two hinged flaps at the top. The flaps, which are also the wings, fold upwards and flat against the metal rod when you push it into the compost.

When you pull the handle upwards, they haul some of the organic materials up and subsequently fold outwards, causing them to stick out from the rod up to an 80-degree angle. A winged aerator requires a considerable amount of strength to operate but is effective for compost piles with minimal moisture and chopped material.

If you can't afford a turner or aerator, you have the option of using a long and thin stick to poke holes in the pile and allow oxygen to get inside. Or you can make your DIY auger-aerator by going to the nearest recreational vehicles supply store and getting an anchor – a tool typically used to secure mobile homes.

The base of the drill has an opening at the top. You just need to stick a piece of wood in the opening to serve as the handle, and you have something to use as both turner and aerator without breaking the bank.

Thermometer

Having a compost thermometer isn't compulsory, but it can solve lots of problems. More importantly, it can eliminate the need for guesswork concerning temperature. A thermometer can't help if you can't get your pile to heat up, but it helps when you need to know how much heat you got in the stack.

A thermometer is a must-have if your composter needs to kill pathogens and seeds effectively to work efficiently. Keep in mind that thermometers can be pretty expensive. Some cost hundreds of dollars, but they are usually designed for large-scale organic composting systems.

All you need for your home composting system is a readable dial with a long probe at its end. A good probe should be about 24" long. Still, most vary from 12" to 72" for backyard compost piles.

You can also consider tying a lengthy ribbon to an oven or an outdoor/indoor thermometer and burying it in your compost pile. Once you've waited sufficiently, just pull the thermometer out by the ribbon to read your compost temperature. Just make sure to protect the thermometer with a plastic bag before you shove it deep into the composting heap.

Note that many oven thermometers don't measure temperatures below 120 degrees, so they may prove to be a limited tool. But generally, they should give a hint of the ballpark you are in.

Screen

If you choose to screen your compost, you will need a screener to do this. You can either buy or build a screener yourself. Before you do that, you have to decide on a screening style. Some growers use a sifter to shake and sift through soil or compost. Others simply press it down through a wire sieve.

Use a small sifter, or you'll be burdened with a needlessly heavy and bulky one. The sifter should have raised sides that will help hold the organic compost in place. Rubbing screeners are pretty large, but they don't require raised sides to sift compost.

Note that a screener may not be necessary if you plan to dig your finished compost directly into your garden beds when you need to. In that case, getting a screener would be a waste of your time and money.

Tarps

Tarps come in handy in organic composting. You can use them to store the materials you accumulate until you have enough to start building a compost heap. They can also be used to mix the organic matter before you put them into the compost bin.

If you don't have a wheelbarrow, you can use the tarps to transport your materials to the composting location. Additionally, you'd also need to spread one tarp under your screener to catch anything that escapes the receptacle during a sifting or screening operation.

Leaf-Shredder

Leaf shredders aren't necessary if you have sufficient space where you can pile up the brown material you collect for your compost pile. Over time, the leaves will begin to break down into compostable material.

However, that may not be an option if you only have a small plot with many trees. Thankfully, shredded materials take up far less space. Using an electric shredder allows you to produce one bag of mulch from several bags of leaves. The good thing is shredded material also decomposes far more quickly, as the shredder has done most of the work.

An electric shredder is your best bet because gas-powered ones contribute heavily to noise and environmental pollution. The average leaf-shredder runs on standard household power, so you don't have to worry about getting a complementary power source.

You can also set it to fine, medium, or coarse shredding. Since it comes with a stand, you can attach a lead bag or tarp underneath or place it atop a garbage can. An electric shredder works for leaves, paper, and pine needles. You can use it to produce a wide range of materials that can go into your compost pile.

Garden Cart or Wheelbarrow

A garden cart or wheelbarrow will prove essential if you have a large yard to generate plenty of compost. It also helps haul compost from one plant to the next, whether your garden is huge or not. Garden carts and wheelbarrows typically come in varying shapes, sizes, and weights. Simply get one that appeals to your taste and preference.

How to Build a Basic DIY Compost Bin

The instructions below describe how to build a movable, wooden compost bin consisting of similar interlocking sections stacked on top of one another. As your compost's volume decreases, you can easily take off the top sections of the bin and use it to build another container. This type of bin is specifically designed to let you adjust its size based on your needs. Don't forget to add polythene or a wooden lid to prevent the rain from beating your pile.

The size of your compost box, according to these instructions, will be 75 x 75 x 75 cm. You can adjust the size according to personal requirements and the available materials. That also means you can build your bin with pallets, floorboards, and other timber materials.

Keep in mind that the size of your compost box can affect the decomposition process positively or negatively. So, you shouldn't build a smaller bin than the recommended size here. Since all interlocking sections are identical, the materials and equipment needed are all the same.

Here are the required materials and equipment for each section:

- 2.5ft wooden board x 2 (3in wide and 0.6in thick)
- 2.4ft wooden board x 2 (3in wide and 0.6in thick)
- 5 x 2in wooden corner blocks x 4 (2.16in long)
- 1.4in screws x 20, size 8
- A saw, screwdriver, and drill

Note that the length and thickness of the boards should remain constant. You may use slightly broader or narrower boards so long as you adjust the corner block sizes to match. If your timber is variable, you don't have to use the same width for all sections of the compost box.

Follow the instructions below to build the box:

1. Cut two boards of 2.5ft length

2. Cut two panels of 2.4ft length

3. From the 5 x 2in lumber, cut 4 x 2.16in lengths to make the corner blocks

4. Take one of the 2.4ft boards and position it on two of the 2.16in pieces. The corner blocks should be flush with the ends of the shorter boards. Ensure the blocks are offset to project them at least 0.8in beyond the board's edge.

5. Hold down the board on the blocks and drill three holes 1.2in deep at either end of the board. Drill through the board into the block and fasten the holes with three screws.

6. Repeat steps 4 and 5 for the other end of the box.

7. Again, repeat steps 4, 5, and 6 with the other 2.4ft board. The next stage might require you to find another person to hold the boards while connecting them.

8. Place the two boards with corner blocks attached to their ends. Make sure they are in an upright position and are 2.5ft apart. The protruding ends should be away from your position.

9. Place one longer board atop the vertical boards to build the third side of the first section. The ends of the 2.5ft boards should be flush with the vertical boards' outer edges.

10. Drill each end of the longer board as explained in step 5 and fasten with two screws this time.

11. Turn the unfinished side upwards and position the second 2.5ft board across the middle of the shorter boards as previously. Place squarely and drill and fasten with screws as in step 9.

You have successfully built the first section of your compost bin. Complete the remaining sections by following the instructions above. Remember that you can make as many sections as required until you meet your desired number of compost bins.

Build a Three-Crate Bin System

The three-crate bin system efficiently creates finished compost in weeks, so it's a favorite among gardeners. If you would like to wait less than months before you can access your very own black gold, this is the system for you.

The compost system is made from rot-resistant cedarwood, and it features front plants and enough space for air movement. The planks are removable. Overall, if built the right way, the three-bin compost system offers a clean look.

Perhaps the best thing about this system is that you can build and set it up in as little as 5 hours. To make the compost bin, you need the following tools:

- One drill
- One measuring tape
- One saw
- One box of 2 ½ inch screws for wood
- One box of 2-inch screws for wood
- One sledgehammer or mallet
- One roll of 36 x 3 feet chicken wire or any other wire netting
- Four four-feet long metal fence posts, with screw holes
- Staple gun and staples

For the wooden material, you need:

- Nine pieces of 1 inch by 6 inches by 10 feet s
- Seven pieces of 1 inch by 6 inches by 12 feet
- Two pieces of 1 inch by 2 inches by 10 feet
- Two pieces of 2 inches by 6 inches by 12 feet
- Two pieces of 2 inches by 4 inches by 12 feet
- Two pieces of 2 inches by 6 inches by 10 feet

Cut the woods according to the following requirements:

- Removable front planks – four of the 1x6x12 pieces into 3 feet 7 ½ inches. Cut a total of 12 planks.

- Side slats – eighteen pieces of 4 foot 6-inch slats from the 1x6x10s.

- Uprights – Eight pieces of 2 foot 10 ½ inch planks from the 2x4x12s for the middle and end panels.

- Bottom – four pieces of 4 foot 9 inches from the 2x6x10s.

- Supports – eight pieces of 2 foot 10 ½ inches from the 2x6x12s for the front and back.

- Supports – six pieces of 2 foot 10 ½ inches from the 1x2x10s for plank support.

- Back slats – the rest of the uncut 1x6x12s.

Follow the instructions below to make the compost box end panels:

- Find a flat surface – place two of the side slats atop two uprights. Drill guide holes before you begin to avoid breaking the wood, then attach them.

- Add another side slat to make a whole side panel. Make sure it's evenly spaced.

- Attach the front and back supports by screwing them into the side slats and the uprights.

- Flip the panel upside down and attach the bottom pieces with the 2 ½ inch wood screws.

- Build the other end panel by repeating steps 1 to 5.

Now, you can build the middle panels by following the same instruction for end panels. But there are a few exceptions:

- Repeat steps 1 and 2 of the end panel above.

- Flip the panels and fasten three additional side slats onto the middle panel.

- Ensure the supports for the front and back are placed perpendicularly to the uprights.

- Attach the bottom pieces to the side slats with the 2 ½ inch screws.

• Join the plank supports and uprights together to make grooves for the planks. Do this for the side panels as well.

Once you've made the end and middle panels, it's time to set up the compost bin. Do that by following the instructions below:

• Set the panels on their supports. Join the 12-foot back slats to the back supports for the end panels.

• Mark the position of the middle panels by measuring 48 to 49 inches from both ends. Join the panels with screws and center marks on the back supports.

• Place one of the bins with bottom pieces on the ground and put four removable planks into each bin. That will help space the front supports evenly.

• Extract the planks, then pound in the metal fence posts. Attach the posts.

• Using the staple gun and staples, attach the wire netting to the insides of the bins.

• Finally, replace the removable front planks.

This system is easy to operate. The key is to fill the first bin with fruits, veggies, wood shavings, newspapers, dry leaves, and other compostables. Whenever it's full, use your turner to turn the organic matter into the second bin every three to four days.

The more frequent the turning, the faster decomposition will take place. After a while, start filling the third bin with new compostable materials. By the time the third bin is full, the compost in the second bin should be ready, and the first bin should be empty, meaning you can start the process all over again.

Chapter Three: Build Your Organic Compost Pile

Before you start building your organic compost, choosing a good location is of the utmost importance. Location is a key factor in the planning process. It increases efficiency and ensures that your surroundings remain tidy. More importantly, it makes the whole process almost effortless.

Ideally, your compost bin should be located in a place where it's both convenient and discreet to yourself and others, such as your neighbors. Usually, the need for convenience and unobtrusiveness often cross each other, but you can easily find a good spot in your backyard.

In most cases, your backyard size will determine where to put your composting bin. However, keep in mind that having a large backyard does not automatically mean you can find a convenient or satisfactory spot.

A small home and backyard might make it easier to pick a location for your compost pile. However, since the available area limits gardening capacity, you'll have fewer location possibilities to choose from.

Your decision will be hugely influenced by whether you want a simple composting system or a properly managed setup. The amount of organic matter you intend to generate should also factor in when making the decision.

At the outset, you might not be sure about the level of commitment you'll have for composting. In that case, consider starting with a small site in your garden where you can set up a simple compost system. That'd allow you to easily upgrade whenever you feel like you are ready to advance. The good thing is there is no escaping becoming an avid composter once you start reaping the benefits of using compost you made by yourself. Nothing is more satisfying.

A compost pile remains in the same location for years, so you have to choose your location with some forethought. If you plan to build a conventional heap, your best bet is to keep it close enough to your house.

The most logical thing to do is choose an existing related zone, such as your greenhouse or kitchen. Doing that will make carrying scraps from your kitchen to the pile less of a chore. Regardless of the size and system you choose for your organic composting operation, the ideal choice is to ensure it's close to a garden-related zone in your home. That is the best way to ensure ease of access.

Also, the ability to see the compost location from your house means you'll be aware of and when marauders start visiting the pile. That means you won't need to stake out your backyard just to catch the offender in action.

Now, since compost piles don't precisely add aesthetic value to your home, you might want to build yours in an area that's out of view. Do not choose a location where the pile will dominate the view from your windows.

Remember that composting can affect your relationship with your neighbors, especially over the look or smell. Therefore, choosing an area where the pile won't obstruct others' views as well is important. You should also maintain the pile well enough to prevent it from developing an unpleasant odor. Don't worry, because we'll cover that later down the line.

Since you'll need to water your compost pile occasionally, the ideal location should be near a good water source. On the other hand, heavy rains can potentially wash all the nutrients out of the pile. So, if you don't plan to keep it covered, ensure you build it under a where it can be spared all possible deluges. It is advisable to provide your bin or pile with adequate covering instead of relying on nature to prevent overwatering. A lid or protective roof should do the trick.

You can start composting with a small bin outside your backyard door while you educate yourself more about the whole process. Should you decide to do that, you won't be needing a lot of space.

However, if you plan to set up a full-on composting operation in your garden, you need to remember to leave extra space to carry out necessary maintenance tasks.

In a single compost bin system, the size of your pile should be relative to your yard's size, or the vessel meant for composting. The bin or tumbler is a depository for organic waste from your garden, so it's only natural to ensure the size is in scale with the property.

Simply put, the smaller your yard, the smaller the organic matter–twigs, leaves, weeds, clippings–that is generated. Therefore, the size of your compost system should match the number of materials you think your yard can generate.

Of course, it's not easy to estimate the eventual size of a compost heap when you first start. Since the bin gradually sinks as the organic matter at its base begins to decompose, the eventual size might escape your estimation.

With this fact in mind from the beginning, you should find it easier to evaluate the amount of space needed for your composting system. The dimensions will remain constant from season to season after the initial guesswork.

Regardless of your estimated space, always add at least 6' on each side for your pile. That leaves enough room to store a garden cart or wheelbarrow and any tools required to turn and help maintain the pile. Turning a compost pile requires a little elbow room.

Single piles usually pose a few location challenges since they are stationary. You may need to use a compost starter to jumpstart and accelerate the decomposition process. Compared to managed piles, single piles tend to stay in the same location for years. Therefore, choosing the best spot from the start is crucial.

Now, suppose your goal is to produce huge amounts of organic compost. In that case, you need to do more than recycle your household waste and gardening matter. What that means is you'll need significant space for the composting operation.

To produce compost efficiently on a somewhat larger scale, you need an adequate supply of green and brown materials, as explained in the first chapter. You need enough materials to build three piles with measurements that are between 3x3x3 to 5x5x5 feet.

Since green and brown waste materials are typically abundant throughout different seasons, you must allocate space to store them separately until it's time to compost. Usually, autumn leaves can be stored in bags to compost in spring when you'll have fresh grass clippings, weeds, and pruning tips.

Additionally, you might decide to import organic material from outside your home if your garden doesn't provide enough. In that case, be sure to allocate space to accommodate the manure, wood chips, straws, grass clippings, and other organic waste from external sources. It would be wise to invest in a container if you plan to use manure to avoid foul odor.

Since you need to turn managed bins more times than single compost bins, consider extra capacity in the planning. Again, this means you should add in 6' to 8' around the sides of your bins, so you can have adequate space to turn, replenish, and harvest.

Pick a spot in the composting area to store essential tools and equipment, and most importantly, keep them dry. Refer back to chapter two for information on all the tools to get before you start composting.

Apart from equipment and tool storage, plan out a designated space to shred and chop your materials if needed. It's recommended to build two piles – one for materials that are yet to be shredded and another for materials ready for the compost heap.

If you don't use all the finished compost immediately after production, store it properly in another bin, a trash can, or leave it as a pile for future use. Since ready compost rarely produces an odor (if properly kept), you may decide to store it near your garden or greenhouse. Otherwise, just find a suitable spot for it in your composting zone.

You might be wondering if your compost bin should be set up in the sun or shade. It does not matter whether the location is sunny or shady – neither sun nor shade has a significant impact on the decomposition process.

The heat contributing to composting is typically generated by the organic contents rather than the pile's exposure to sunlight. And that's why it doesn't matter if you go for hot or cold composting.

Naturally, if you put the pile in a sunny area, the sun is certain to dry out its outer layers, especially if you don't enclose it in a bin. But this problem mostly occurs in regions with hot, arid climates, in which case you'll need to take steps to prevent dehydration. However, a specific amount of shade in the composting area will make the work more bearable and easier for you in the summer heat. Remember overheating the pile can reverse all the hard work you've put into it so far.

Another thing to factor in when choosing the perfect location is wind. When you turn your compost, you'll be stirring up plenty of dust and debris. So, it's not advisable to choose a location that is susceptible to the wind.

Strong wind exposure does not help the composting process in any way. Whatever aeration advantage you get from good airflow caused by a windy spot is negated by the tendency of the pile to dry out without an equally decent source of water.

Suppose you can't avoid the strong wind no matter the location you choose. In that case, consider getting temporary plastic sheeting or a tarp to cover up the pile in case the outer layers start to dry out. You would also do well to spray it with some water to increase the moisture content before you cover it up.

Earlier, it was mentioned that you could build your compost pile near or under a tree to protect it from deluges. Well, this doesn't work with all kinds of trees. Most of the time, it's better to have an overhanging deciduous tree to protect your compost from the summer sun and still leave enough room for sunshine to come through during fall.

That can help the organic pile sustain its temperature for an extended period into winter. Although trees may be considered a blessing in composting, their proximity can make it difficult to choose a good location for your compost bin.

If you aren't careful, the trees' underground roots may begin growing towards the compost soil surface while the nutrient-rich humus is getting ready in the base of the composting pile. The roots often do this in the quest for nutrients, but some feeder roots go as far as the top 12' of the soil and extend as far as the soil's surface for air.

Some trees have more aggressive roots than others, meaning they infiltrate compost piles more quickly. Black lotus, Eucalyptus, Redwood, Ailanthus, Willow, and Alder are trees with very aggressive roots. If you have any of these in your backyard, make sure you don't put your compost heap near it.

If your only or preferred option is near any of the trees mentioned above, build your pile on a raised wooden platform. That way, you can separate the pile from the soil and prevent the roots from hijacking the compost nutrients.

You can also put the pile on scrap metal sheets, concrete pads, or in a bin with a plastic base. Generally, though, it's better to use a bin with a vented base to enable air circulation. Consider a purpose-made bin, wooden pallet, or cinder blocks.

Another way to discourage tree roots from migrating into your heap is to move the bin periodically. Do this with your storage material as well. Change the location of your pile every time you start a new one.

The distance between your compost bin and house is important. Although, as previously noted, it's ideal to choose a close spot to your kitchen and garden to allow for convenient movement from one spot to another. Ideally, though, your pile should be 10 feet away from your house, at the very least. It's also important to set it up in a downwind position. Be careful not to put the pile up against any building, fence, or wall, as this can limit air circulation. Air must flow to all sides of the heap.

Additionally, if the wall you put it up against is made of wooden material, the decomposing organisms can rot the wall. In just a short period, the accumulated moisture and weight of the pile can damage the wooden surface.

Don't forget to ensure that your state or local area permits home composting before you start planning and setting the system up.

Compost Materials

Once you've decided on a suitable location, the next step is to choose appropriate brown and green materials to add to the heap. In chapter one, you learned briefly about the dos and don'ts of compost materials.

The question most beginners ask is, "What can I compost?" The right question, though, should be, "What can't I compost?" It's much more helpful to be familiar with the materials that should never make it into your pile since you can compost almost anything that was once alive.

You already know that compost materials are categorized into "green" and "brown" to simplify the process. As explained earlier, "green" compostables are materials with higher nitrogen content.

They are usually young and succulent. "Brown" materials, in contrast, have higher carbon contents, as they come from older plants and/or materials.

The best time to collect brown compostables is during late summer and fall when they are usually readily available. Collect the leaves in your garden in the fall and store them in a bag or a place where you can easily cover them with a tarp. Remember that it's crucial to keep the rain out.

If you are in a rural or suburban area where you can readily access straw bales, it is recommended to carry and store one away in the fall. Then, add to your pile when needed throughout the rest of the seasons. Straw bales make good brown material for a compost pile.

As previously explained, there is a ratio of carbon-to-nitrogen materials that can go into a pile. The costliest mistake you can make when building your pile is having more nitrogen materials than carbon ones.

It's easy to use too many green materials when your kitchen and greenhouse provide a steady supply of them. Moreover, carbon materials are mostly available in the summer and fall. But remember that your pile can potentially turn aerobic if you use too many greens. In turn, this can cause an unpleasant odor, pest problems, and nutrient loss.

If ever you happen to make a mistake with your pile, make sure the mistake is to have too many brown materials *rather than green ones.* With an overabundance of high-carbon materials, the worst that can happen is for heating to slow down in the pile. That prolongs the decomposition process slightly and makes it harder to get finished compost.

The list of compostable materials is endless. Apart from the materials listed in chapter one, many others are suitable for composting. Normally, you can compost materials of all kinds from various types of plants. Still, the key is to make the pile as varied and diverse as possible. It may take a while to gather materials actively, but you'll find it to be worth the effort.

Compost materials can include anything from the leaves of a plant to its roots and stalks. As plants age, they go through certain stages, which can affect your compost positively. When considering what to add to the pile, you should remember that each part of a plant contributes something different.

To understand this, you should be familiar with what plants experience as they age.

• Young plants have higher nitrogen and glucose content. They are juicy and succulent. In a pile, they are the first to break down and even act as accelerants to boost the bacterial population and accumulate heat more rapidly. Having them in your pile is a no-brainer.

• As plants start to grow and form stalks, they synthesize complex carbs to ensure long-term growth. In a pile, they break down for a longer period, but they also give the pile more energy when it eventually decomposes. That alone increases the compost heat considerably.

• Like humans, plants also stiffen with age. They become stiff by producing cellulose and lignin in their stems to gain the rigidity required to support branches, flowers, leaves, and fruit.

In several plants, older leaves tend to synthesize phenols as a way of keeping pests away. Some synthesize waxy cuticles to retain more moisture and keep diseases from infecting them. In a compost heap, the cellulose, phenols, lignin, and waxes are probably the most resistant to decomposition.

If your pile's size is big enough, heat rises to where the cellulose can't help but break down, resulting in a significant energy release.

In summary, it's important to have materials of all types and ages from various kinds of plants in your pile. The young, green materials will kick-start the process and keep the pile going, while middle-aged and older plant clippings will provide the bulk with much-needed energy for the heating phase. Finally, the roots will increase the humic content of your ready compost.

The diversity of compost ingredients is the best way to produce bio-diversified compost.

The carbon-to-nitrogen ratio, as previously defined, is the balance between green and brown materials in a compost pile. Green materials help build the bodies of the billions of organisms that break down the organic matter while carbon fuels their growth with energy.

Green compostables have a lower C: N ratio because they contain more nitrogen, while brown ones have a higher C: N ratio since they contain more carbon.

The C: N ratio is crucial because it guides you on balancing carbon and nitrogen in your pile. Growers consider the ability to strike the perfect balance an art. But the fact is it is as much a science as it is art.

To understand how to use ingredients in proportion to one another, you should know the C: N ratio of the compost materials you put in your compost. Where you have a range in the ratio, follow the midpoint when estimating proportions.

For example, if a certain ingredient has a high C: N ratio like 400:1, ensure you add it in small amounts and thin layers. Then, blend it with another material with a low C: N material.

Your compost should contain more materials with high C: N ratios. With just enough nitrogen content, these break down more readily in piles.

Over time, you will develop experience and develop a sense of what materials you should use, as well as what works in your compost pile. The point of the C: N ratio is to give you an excellent starting point. Again, you should refer back to chapter one for information on what to and what not to compost.

Composting Methods

Layering is a vital aspect of organic composting and the most widespread composting method. It is recommended for beginners who want to produce their homemade compost quickly. The way you layer your materials can affect the maturing period before you get finished compost. Therefore, it's important to get your layering right. There is no better method to start a pile than layering.

Think of it as making lasagna – you add thin layers of the same materials in a recurring pattern. After the pile is activated, you can add new ingredients into the middle of the heap or incorporate them during turning.

The first layer should be between 6 to 8 inches and contain brown and green organic matter. Ensure you add the materials thinly, as packing them onto each other can restrict airflow and oxygen, which the decomposing bacteria need.

In the second layer, you should add a starter or activator material such as fertilizers, manure, etc. Since you can't just add any type of activator, more will be explained on the acceptable types in the next chapter. The starters are meant to hasten the process – they heat the pile and achieve the required temperature by releasing much-needed nitrogen for the microorganisms.

The third layer should contain a 1 to 2-inch layer of finished compost or topsoil. You need this to attract necessary bacteria, fungi, and other organisms to the pile. Ensure you don't use sterile topsoil or one that was recently treated with insecticides.

Layering aside, there are other ways to build your compost pile. Some of these methods are:

• **Laissez-faire:** This is probably the most straightforward composting method. It involves dumping all your compostables into the heap and simply walking away. This approach is pretty satisfactory for anyone without a specific timeframe. However, you may find it difficult to keep the heap neat. Plus, finished compost may be harder to access, which makes the pile susceptible to going anaerobic.

• **Sheet Composting:** This method requires you to spread compostable materials over a garden plot or dig them into the top layer of your soil. It is best done in the fall, which means most ingredients will have decayed by planting season as long as you don't include large wooden items. In this case, either stick to leaves and twigs or shred the material if necessary.

• **In-Situ Pile:** Since the endgame is to dig finished compost into your garden, this method starts from the jump. Instead of gathering materials and hauling them to the bin and back to your garden, you can just compost them in the garden. This method might not be for you if you plan to eliminate your kitchen scraps with small-scale composting. But if you have a big enough garden to accommodate a pile and you get the bulk of your ingredients from the garden, you should have no problem using this approach. It just depends on how close or far away your garden is from your home.

• **Trench Composting** involves building your pile in a trench right in your garden plot and then planting directly around the trench. Since decomposing microbes need nitrogen, which will be unavailable to plants as long as the microorganisms are using it, you can bury the trench for as long as a year before you start planting in its vicinity.

There are other methods, but those are the most effective and foolproof ones to try. As previously noted, layering is the most recommended for beginners because it is the easiest and quickest method to get matured compost. So, consider starting your journey with this method.

Steps to Building a Compost Pile

Follow the step-by-step instructions below to build your compost pile practically:

1. Wet the chosen compost area a day or two before you begin building the pile, then again before the actual assembly. The point of this is to awaken the dormant bacteria and fungi in the soil, and more importantly, prepare the soil to accommodate the floor organisms that will soon find their way into the pile. Keep in mind that these organisms are crucial players in the composting process.

2. Start the first layer with coarse, brown materials such as straw. Dry, stalky debris is some of the best to have at the base of a compost heap. Not only do they resist compaction, but they also provide room for the air at the bottom of the pile.

3. Spread a few handfuls of loose topsoil over the first layer to inoculate the heap with vital soil microbes. Alternatively, scatter a compost activator, but know that microbes in your environment are adapted to your garden soil over external sources. Therefore, the soil gives them a better chance at survival.

4. Wet the soil or activator down with a spray of water. Use a "shower" setting on the hose to ensure the materials in your pile are wet but not soaked.

5. Add another layer consisting of green materials this time. This should add a sufficient amount of nitrogen to the base of the pile. Kitchen scraps and green, leafy materials from your garden will work just fine as well.

6. Next, add a thin layer of linden, valley oak, or any compostable dried tree leaves. Trees absorb minerals from deep in the subsoil and bring them to the surface when leaves fall. Composting dried tree leaves is a way of siphoning the minerals into your pile. Ensure you add them in thin layers as tree leaves

tend to become slimy mats when layered into a pile or onto each other thickly.

7.   Wet the layer again. Realistically, a compost pile should have around a 50% moisture level, which is about the moisture level of a wrung-out sponge. If you dig in and squeeze a handful of compost, you shouldn't get more than two drops of water. The easiest way to achieve the desired moisture level is to wet each layer slightly as you build your pile. Don't use more than a quick spray from the water wand on the green layer, but add more water to brown layers since they are thicker.

8.   Spread a "microbial inoculant," i.e., a few handfuls of quality topsoil over each layer you add, to inject the pile with the familiar soil microbes that are best suited to your garden's conditions. If you don't trust the effectiveness of your soil, use a compost activator instead.

9.   Again, add another layer of green materials to increase the nitrogen content. This will awaken the microbes that are in the topsoil you sprinkled onto the previous layer.

10.   Add another layer of brown materials.

11.   Add a thin layer of tree leaves again.

12.   Once you've built the compost pile up to a third of the way, add another nitrogen-heavy layer as a way to generate heat. Be careful not to add too much. Just a little more nitrogen at this stage enhances the breakdown process throughout the entire pile. This is because the materials on top will retain heat from this layer, giving room for the overall temperature of the pile to increase.

13.   Spread a few handfuls of old compost, if you have any. Use garden soil if you don't. Mix the high-nitrogen matter into the layer with a composting fork. Dissolve some compost activator inside water and use it to wet this layer. Or use ordinary water if your inoculant is ordinary garden soil. Ensure the layer

isn't too moist but contains enough water content. This is the point where heat starts rising in the pile, so it's important to get the moisture level right.

14.   Add another layer of brown matter and water the layer.

15.   Add more layers of tree leaves and green materials. Remember to wet each layer before adding another one. Also, adjust the amount of water you add to match the compost materials' moisture level.

The key is to keep alternating green and brown materials in layers as you build the compost pile. Remember that it's crucial to add a compost activator to every layer you add. More importantly, water each layer.

After you've built the pile to the top, wet the surface down with water and cover it up with a tarp. The tarp helps to keep excess moisture out when it rains and retains moisture inside the pile even when the weather is hot and dry. It also keeps the loose materials on top of the heap intact in case it gets windy.

Turning and Aerating Your Compost Pile

The best and only way to get as much compost as you want in the shortest period is to turn and aerate your pile according to its requirements. At the basic level, the benefits you get from turning your pile boil down to aeration.

Microbes are responsible for decomposition, but they can't make it happen if there isn't enough air supply for them to thrive. They need oxygen to function. Without enough oxygen, the microbes in your compost heap will die off, and decomposition may completely stop.

Many things can create an anaerobic (oxygen-free) environment in a pile. Fortunately, most of the problems associated with under oxygenation can be solved or greatly reduced by consistently turning your compost pile. Some of these problems include:

- **High Moisture Content:** If the moisture level in a pile is too high, the tiny pockets between particles become filled with water instead of air. Turning drains the water and makes sure that those pockets become air pockets.

- **Compaction:** This is when the particles in a pile become too close to each other, leaving little room for air. It is the most obvious way to use turning to aerate a pile. Turning will fluff the heap, creating pockets for oxygen to get inside the compost and supply the decomposing microbes.

- **Overconsumption:** When you keep the microbes in your pile happy, they may become overenthusiastic. That pushes them to do their job too well. The microbes closest to the pile's center may consume all the oxygen and nutrients they require for survival and then die off. By turning the compost, you can mix up the pile, which means un-depleted materials and healthy microbes will be moved back to the center of the heap. That will invariably keep the process running.

- **Overheating:** Sometimes, overheating occurs in a compost heap. This is somewhat similar to overconsumption because it happens when the microbes do their jobs too well. The overenthusiasm causes them to produce too much heat, killing them when the temperature becomes way higher than needed. Turning the compost will redistribute the hot compost throughout the pile into cooler, outer areas. That will keep the temperature in the pile within the ideal range for the decomposition process. Additionally, make sure to protect your pile from any secondary heat source, i.e., the sun.

As a home gardener, your aerating options are limited. You can turn manually with a fork, shovel, or aerator, or you can go the automatic way by using a composting tumbler instead of a basic composting bin. Both of these methods work equally well for aeration.

Compost tumblers come as a complete unit, which means you only need to turn the barrel as frequently as needed. For an open compost pile in a single bin system, you can turn the bin by digging your fork or shovel into the heap and manually turning it over a few times. If you have a double or triple bin system, you can easily turn the pile by transferring it from one bin to the next.

How often you turn your compost depends on some factors, including the C: N ratio, the size of your pile, and the moisture level in the pile. Given that, a general rule of thumb is to turn the pile every 3-7 days. In a tumbler, you should do it every 3-4 days.

The more your compost matures, the less frequently you need to turn your pile. However, there are some signs to watch out for, letting you know if you need to turn your pile more frequently. Some include pest infestation, slow decomposition, and smelly piles.

Note that turning your pile when it starts to smell can worsen the smell initially, as you release the trapped gases from the center of the pile. So, keep the direction of the wind in mind in case this happens.

Building a compost pile from scratch should pose no problem if you carefully follow all the steps and tips outlined in this chapter.

Chapter Four: Speeding Up the Process with Organic Activators

When you start composting, you might notice that your organic matter isn't turning into compost after some weeks. In searching for a solution to the slow decomposition problem, you will come across "compost activators," which are catalysts to make your organic waste decompose faster.

However, you don't have to do this if you already know about activators and use them in your pile. You might be wondering why you need activators if you just use a balance of carbon and nitrogen ingredients, as explained. Well, you're about to find out.

First, an activator is an additive that you combine with your organic matter to begin and speed up the composting process. Decomposition happens due to the billions of microbes that work hard to break down your organic matter.

Anything organic will eventually decompose if you give it enough time. But you can make things happen more quickly by striking the correct balance of the main composting elements: Carbon, nitrogen, oxygen, and water.

The key is to create the ideal conditions for important microbial activities to develop more quickly and allow the microorganisms to do their job. Yet, that is where things tend to get slightly tricky.

Most growers, especially beginners, don't know how to balance green and brown materials in a compost pile. The fact is that it's not as easy as it appears to be. The availability of both brown and green materials varies throughout the year, meaning a steady supply of both all year round is hard to come by.

Insufficient nitrogen is the one ingredient that can slow down decomposition. High-nitrogen materials are what bacteria need to break down organic matter. Without sufficient nitrogen, they can't do their part, which leads to the need for compost activators.

Most activators are rich in nitrogen, meaning you can feed the bacteria and achieve balance by adding said activators to your compost heap.

Another thing that may necessitate activators is the lack of microbial diversity in your new pile. Realistically, all organic matter you add to your compost bin already contains millions of microbes. Still, it's common practice to introduce new microbes to the pile as a way to bio-diversify. This is bacterial supplementation and is referred to as inoculation.

There are compost activators, accelerators, and starters. Unfortunately, most people use these terms interchangeably, which can be problematic. Albeit it's difficult to define and differentiate them clearly, but the main difference between them is usually the ingredients each substance comprises.

Whether you are getting a compost accelerator, starter, or activator, know that they all come in various types. Some can be procured naturally within the comfort of your home. Others are artificial and easy to find in stores.

Natural Activators

Natural activators refer to organic green materials that contain high nitrogen levels. You can use them to get the correct C: N ratio for your garden. The best thing is they can be easily sourced in your garden. Know that not all greens have the nitrogen content required to be a "natural activator."

So here are some of the natural activators you'll find around you:

• Green plants such as grass clippings, alfalfa, comfrey, nettles, and clover.

• Powdered blood and bone meals can be conventionally scattered on organic waste and scraps every time you add them to the compost bin. Other powdered products you can add include soybean, alfalfa, and cottonseed meal.

• Fresh or dry matured manure from animals such as rabbits, chickens, pigs, cows, or even alpacas. It's best to rest the manure for at least a season before using it as a compost activator because fresh manure can destroy leaves and plant roots. You may also use horse manure, but it tends to contain undigested seeds and insecticides capable of negatively affecting the microbes in your pile. You can add manure as a thin layer in the cool composting method, but be sure to cover it with brown materials.

• Coffee grounds have rich nitrogen content, while coffee chaff contains even more nitrogen, meaning you can use them as compost activators. They may be added to cold composting systems readily, or smaller amounts to every green layer in a hot pile. Experts recommend mixing in some lime with the grounds or chaff.

• Human urine may also be used as an organic activator for compost due to its ability to speed up decomposition. Urine contains relatively low nitrogen content and 98% water, meaning it is readily available for the microorganisms in a compost pile. It is most effective in dry composting systems. Diluted urine makes it difficult for compost to dry out.

You also have artificial or commercial compost activators referred to as "compost boosters" and "super compost activators."

There are wide ranges of commercially available activators, and you can get them in an online or local store in your area. Just make sure you research a brand before purchasing the activator. Garotta, DOFF, and Vitax are some of the brands recommended for your compost bin.

Microbes and Enzyme Activators

This is also referred to as an inoculant. It is the type of activator that provides supplementary microbes to enhance decomposition. Enzyme activators are dissolved in water and sprinkled on organic matter to "awaken" or "activate" the composting microorganisms.

The addition of an inoculant at the right stage of decomposition speeds up the process and increases the temperature in the pile. This kind of activation helps cool composting systems where the organic content is less likely to have a balanced C: N ratio.

Finished compost is considered the best type of inoculant. If you have any compost from another pile, just sprinkle a handful or thin layer on every 10 to 12 inches of new organic matter. This will introduce new microbes and insects to the pile.

If you have never tried composting, you might not have any spare finished compost. In that case, you can add your garden soil or topsoil. While this may not have as many nutrients as finished compost, there is a mass of microbes that can help inoculate your pile.

Some people consider the use of inoculants unnecessary. Some argue that adding extra microbes to a compost pile with an organic activator makes no significant difference. The argument is that organic matter already contains millions of organisms which will multiply as the bin conditions improve.

There are commercially available inoculants that contain microbes instead of nutrients, which are also regarded as compost activators. They often include a blend of helpful bacteria, fungi, and enzymes. They are said to enhance decomposition and boost the quality of the finished compost by adding beneficial microbes to increase the activity of those already in the pile.

There are specially formulated inoculants for specific purposes. For instance, you have degrading lignin fungi applied to woody materials to significantly reduce the amount of time required to produce nutrient-rich compost suited for growing annual plants. Some are also used to make fungal dominant finished compost which is more suited for perennial plants.

You can purchase compost activators or make some by yourself. That decision is yours to make. However, homemade activators may be better since you mix the ingredients manually. That way, you can easily formulate the perfect blend, depending on the needs of your pile.

How to Get DIY Compost Activators

Before we get to how to produce homemade activators, you should know that they aren't recommended if you plan to depend on a tumbler and kitchen scraps for your compost heap. The DIY boosters mentioned here are rich nitrogen sources best used for large piles with dead leaves, weeds, etc., from your yard.

1.   Supermarket Waste

If you go to any grocery store and ask for their past-date products nicely, they might give them to you. But not all supermarkets give away old or expired produce. It's best to ask at independent local stores and regional chains. The produce typically contains nitrogen nutrients, so all you need to do is throw them into the pile, and they will naturally boost the composting process for you.

2.   Beer Activator

This is a concoction you make from water, beer, ammonia, and sugary soda. If done properly, it can serve as a decent compost starter or activator. You will need the following ingredients:

- Two gallons of water
- One medium-size bottle of beer
- A can of sugary soda
- ½ a cup of ammonia

Simply mix all the ingredients mentioned above in a container and use a watering can to water your fresh compostables with the concoction. Although there is no hard scientific evidence to support the efficiency of this method, many growers assert that it is indeed potent.

The theory is that one of the ingredients contains yeast, which, as you may already know, is a type of fungi. The fungi which normally develop in a compost heap help break down tough carbon materials like corn stalks or branches. So, the fungi from the yeast in the beer do the same thing.

Furthermore, the ammonia in the concoction is quite high in nitrogen, which is why it's used to tend to alkaline-loving garden plants. On the other hand, soda contains a high sugar content (glucose) that can serve as a food source for the microbial population in the pile.

While there is no evidence supporting the assertion that sugar helps decomposition, it's worth giving it a try since the sugar can't negatively affect the compost in any way.

If you want to switch things up, you can swap the ammonia with urea and the beer with actual yeast. Be careful not to add too much urea to prevent your plants from burning out after compost application.

Chapter Five: Hot or Cold Composting

In a previous chapter, you learned that there are two methods of composting: Hot and Cold. Well, there is a midway point between both methods, referred to as warm composting. It helps to have extensive information on all three methods before deciding on a specific one for your pile.

You should know how each can be used to improve garden soil, making growing easier and healthier for your plants. So, one by one, let's discuss these three composting methods and the key factors that differentiate them from one another.

Hot composting is regarded as the quickest way of turning your organic matter into nutrient-filled soil, but it requires plenty of attention and maintenance. Cold composting, on the other hand, requires minimal effort to build and maintain. However, unlike hot composting, it takes a longer time to develop into usable compost.

Both composting methods have advantages and disadvantages, which will be explored throughout this chapter. The good thing is most composting problems are relatively easy to address and solve.

Understandably, some gardeners prefer hot composting while others swear by cold composting. You may be thinking that one method is better than the other, but the truth is it all boils down to your specific needs.

If you choose, you can compromise by meeting somewhere in the middle and settle for a warm compost pile. Although warm composting has only recently become more common, it's just as effective as hot and cold composting,

No matter which one you settle on, the result is usually worth the effort and time. You are sure to have a potent source of nourishing nutrients for your plants to thrive so long as you stick to the guidelines.

You should consider certain things before you choose a composting method. The best way to do that is to establish why you are making compost in the first place. Some of the things to factor in are:

• Do you want nutrient-rich compost to enhance the fertility of your garden soil and reduce your fertilizer use?

• Do you want to keep your garden neat?

• Do you generate regular amounts of food scraps and waste all year round or only get seasonal waste?

• Do you want to improve your ecological footprint and do your part for the environment?

The answer to these questions can help you decide the right composting method for you.

Hot Composting

Hot composting typically takes 4 to 12 weeks to produce usable compost due to the optimized microbial activity. While the process requires time, effort, and some special equipment, it is relatively straightforward. This method is right for anyone who wants to produce compost in the shortest time for immediate use.

The best time to practice your hot composting skill is during late summer. There are plenty of materials to experiment with, and the warm temperature contributes to the process by restricting temperature loss during the nightly temperature drop.

Hot composting finishes with far fewer seeds than cold composting and also has greater volume. Additionally, it tends to contain richer nutrients which help to promote healthier plant growth. Another reason to like hot composting is that it leaves room for a regular full-body workout since you have to turn the compost every 3 to 5 days to keep the process going.

Normally, most gardeners make layers of leaves, dead plants, mulches, and other high-nitrogen green materials when building a compost pile. However, with hot composting, you don't layer your compostable materials. Instead, you mix them after shredding them into smaller pieces.

When building your hot compost pile, make sure it is at least a 4x4 foot space. Size is important in hot composting. If the pile is too small, it won't heat up as it should. Bigger is generally considered better, but 4 feet by 4 feet is ideal for most gardeners.

If possible, place your hot compost pile in full fun. Shade can slow down the process by cooling the pile down. Usually, you can add organic matter to your compost heap until you have accumulated enough, but with hot composting, you must have all the required materials at hand to pile in one go.

That means you need huge amounts of organic matter, which should have the right carbon-to-nitrogen ratio from the beginning. A good rule of thumb is ensuring your organic matter is 30 parts carbon to one nitrogen. Hot composting requires you to shred and chop up whatever material you add to the compost pile, no matter what kind it is. That is the only way to ensure a faster decomposition rate.

Remember that microbial activity is most optimal in hot composting. The two keys to achieving optimization are regular turning and constant monitoring of the soil temperature and moisture content.

The optimal temperature to optimize microbial activity is between 130- and 140-degrees Fahrenheit. You can monitor your pile with a compost or soil thermometer. Alternatively, if you don't get grossed out too easily, you can stick your hand into the pile to check the temperature. If you do that and it's uncomfortably hot, that means you have the right temperature for hot composting.

With a properly balanced carbon and nitrogen content, the microbes will consume all the energy in the center of the heap, causing a drop in temperature. Due to this, you need to turn your hot compost pile at least once a week. That will give the organisms access to fresh air and bring more organic matter from the outer layer of the pile into the center.

The moisture content in a hot compost pile should be moist but not soggy. After about a month, you should have dark and crumbly compost that looks like chocolate cake crumbs. There should be no recognizable remnants of the composted materials.

At that point, the heap should have stopped heating up even when you turn it. However, you still need one or two weeks for curing. That gives room for fresh beneficial microbes to repopulate the pile for new compost.

Speed is one reason why many gardeners choose hot composting over cold composting. Finished compost is available in as little as three weeks with the use of this method. Another reason is that it reduces your spatial needs. Hot compost finishes in a short period, while cold compost can take years to mature properly.

With hot composting, you get full control over your finished product. You can adjust the decomposition speed or temperature by simply turning and aerating the pile. The key is to consider the pile monitoring an art rather than a chore.

Sterilization also makes hot composting more appealing to many gardeners. As the temperature inside the heap increases, weed seeds and pathogens automatically die, meaning the pile loses any harmful effects. That is enough reason for a gardener to choose hot composting since it means your finished compost can't cause damage to your plants.

Hot composting neutralizes harmful pesticides and chemicals present in organic material. Therefore, toxic degradation is a good reason to choose hot composting, especially if you want to make sure that toxins from your compost don't make it to your garden plants.

Most pests leave a hot pile alone, assuming the decomposition process works correctly. On the other hand, if a pile is poorly made, it will attract all kinds of pests, from small ones like ants to bigger mammals like raccoons. Finally, you can use the heat from a well-made compost pile to work by using it to heat your greenhouse, in case you have one.

The above are all pros of hot composting. In addition, they explain why you should choose the hot composting method for your new pile. But what about the reasons to avoid hot composting?

The first is that a hot compost pile is much more difficult to set up than a cold one. If a pile refuses to heat up, it can start smelling and attracting flies. The key to avoiding this is to make your heap in summer so that the natural temperature can give you a head start on the composting process.

A hot compost pile is not to be built in layers or stages. You need all your essential materials on the ground and in the appropriate balance from day one. Gathering materials can be challenging, especially for those starting their composting journey.

Many people ask why hot composting is popular and widely advocated if it has no natural equivalent. It seems that most of the natural composting that happens in the wild is achieved through the cold method.

Overheating can make you lose valuable nutrients and microbes in hot composting and could sometimes even kill off the necessary microorganisms needed. First, you need to check for strong odors or vapor clouds rising from the pile. That is usually a sign that all the valuable nutrients in the compost heap escape into the air. Some experienced gardeners argue that temperatures below 150 degrees can cause significant nutrient loss.

While it isn't a common occurrence, overheating sometimes spontaneously causes combustion in a hot compost pile. This problem is easy to avoid. Simply monitor the temperature in your pile and make sure it goes no higher than 150 degrees Fahrenheit. Also, ensure the pile does not contain pockets of dry materials. If wood ashes are part of your materials, make sure they completely cool off before introducing them into the pile.

Conclusively, the main reason why many gardeners prefer hot composting is the fast results. However, in exchange for this singular benefit, you must be willing to devote considerable time, effort, and attention to your composting activities.

If you are a busy gardener and you don't think you can live up to the expectations, it's okay to turn towards cold composting instead. If, however, you are ready to commit, you will find hot composting effective, rewarding, and satisfactory.

Cold Composting

Gardeners who prefer cold composting do so for entirely different reasons. It is easy to start a cold pile because you can use just about any acceptable materials that you have on hand. And with a cold pile, you don't have to worry about achieving the proper balance of green and brown materials. That is not vital for your success here. Still, incorporating both brown and green materials into your pile will greatly impact the decomposition process.

Unlike in hot composting, you also don't need to shred or chop up large pieces of material before building the pile. Instead, you have all the time in the world to build up your pile gradually. In addition, composting requires air to inhibit the accumulation of anaerobic bacteria. Therefore, aeration is as important in cold composting as it is in hot composting.

Putting some coarse materials in the center can help with air circulations. Unlike hot composting, less moisture is better, which is why you should dry some soggy materials like wet leaves and grass clippings before adding them to the pile. That will prevent them from sticking together and blocking the air from reaching other parts of the pile. If aerations become a problem in a cold compost pile, just get a fork to turn and drove air holes into the center.

It is important to keep track of the moisture content as decomposition continues. If you live in an area where persistent rains can cause a problem, remember to cover the pile with tarps to prevent drowning and anaerobic decay.

Cold composting progresses very slowly, but how slowly depends on the size of your ingredients, your C: N ratio, and the frequency with which you turn and aerate the pile. These factors also affect the temperature of the pile.

On average, maintenance-free cold piles rarely reach 90 degrees Fahrenheit. Piles that contain high nitrogen materials may get warmer if they are turned periodically. The pile base is usually the first to decay, meaning large high-carbon materials are left intact at the top.

The first reason why many gardeners choose cold composting is its simplicity. Starting a pile and getting it to heat up is probably the most difficult thing in composting. You have to achieve near-perfect conditions to make that happen. But with cold composting, you don't have to be in a rush to get your pile to heat up. Instead, you can build and maintain the pile with ease.

Flexibility is a major advantage in cold composting because you can adapt the pile to your personal needs. For example, if you don't have much to compost, just toss whatever is at hand onto the pile and wait until you get your hands on more materials.

If you don't have the time to turn the pile this month, you can leave it unturned until the following month. And if you would like to cut the process short, you only need to dig out usable compost at the bottom of the compost heap.

Hot composting requires at least 3 feet of organic waste ready to start composting at once, but cold composting does not. However, the material requirements are fewer than any other composting method. This allows you to introduce new materials at your own pace as you accumulate size little by little.

One thing that can quickly frustrate a gardener is trying to heat a compost pile in winter. Cold composting takes that frustration away because it allows for decomposition all year round. Even in cold weather, freeze-thaw cycles automatically contribute to breaking down organic materials.

Understandably, not all gardeners have the time or energy to turn a bulky heap every 3 to 5 days. It is stressful and tasking. With cold composting, you can turn your pile whenever you have the time to spare – even if it is just for 15 to 30 minutes. And if you want, you can pass up on turning throughout the whole process. Just note that the process will take longer the less you turn your pile over.

That makes cold composting an excellent choice for older gardeners who want organic humus but can't afford to try hot composting, money and energy-wise.

Many microbial organisms can survive in lower temperatures deep at the bottom of a cold compost pile. Some of these beneficial microbes survive in moderate temperatures, and they are the ones your garden needs to keep the plants healthy and free from diseases.

Now, there are some reasons why cold composting may not be a compatible method for many gardeners. The first is the space requirement. A cold compost pile can take up space for as many months and years as needed. So, it isn't ideal for a gardener without plenty of backyard space.

Even if you do have enough space, keep in mind that a cold compost pile may not be pleasing to the eyes of many, which can prove to be an issue if you have neighbors. So, it's crucial to find a corner of your yard that is not far from the kitchen and still out of your way.

With frequent turning, cold composting can take between six months and a year. It sometimes takes longer with irregular turning. If you want to produce finished compost in a short amount of time, you are better off with hot composting.

Often, cold piles lose their air circulation ability, causing them to collapse. This is especially common when the pile contains matters that stick together. Unless you aerate it periodically, the pile can develop a stinky bacterial mess that attracts flies and other unwanted pests to your yard. On the other hand, a hot pile is less likely to suffer anaerobic decomposition risk since the frequent turning introduces air to the center of the compost heap.

There is probably nothing pests like more than a cold compost pile. It makes a great tourist attraction for bugs and mammals looking to feed on something and possibly nest in throughout the winter. Therefore, the chances of you having lots of rodents and flies around your cold pile are quite high. However, you can keep larger pests such as stray dogs and raccoons away with proper fencing.

Generally, heat is a vital component in composting. It is needed to break down weed seeds, pathogens, and other residues. However, the cold composting method isn't ideal for decomposing invasive weeds, seed weeds, debris from your garden, lawn, or farm that have been treated with insecticides or other toxic chemicals, and diseased plants.

Nutrient leaching is almost inescapable with cold composting. Depending on how long you let the process go on, nutrients tend to leach out of the heap with rainfall. You can use a composting container or cover the pile with a tarp during wet weather. Doing that will help preserve vital nutrients from washing away. You also have the option of periodically digging out finished humus from the bottom of your pile for immediate use.

Remember, compost decays from the bottom up. While the organic matter at the top of the pile is struggling to break down, chances are there is already mature compost accumulated below. Even when the whole process is finished, there might be large pieces remaining, leaving you with a coarser finished product than you will get from hot composting.

Conclusively, the reason for you to choose the cold composting method is that it is as low-maintenance as any busy gardener desires. Another thing is that the quality of finished products from a cold compost pile is more natural.

Furthermore, cold composting fosters more of the beneficial microbes that are necessary for plant health and growth. Properly managed under the right conditions, the product may even have more nutrients than hot compost.

Be careful not to add any ingredient that contains diseased organisms, chemicals, or weed seeds to your cold pile, as these contaminants will perpetuate in decomposition. If you have any doubts about the ingredients you have, discard them or try hot composting instead.

Don't forget that time is a huge factor in cold composting. You can try this method if you don't mind waiting several months for usable compost. However, if you want something to amend and improve your soil quickly, you will benefit more from the hot composting method.

Warm Composting

As explained, warm composting is a hybrid of hot and cold composting. A warm compost pile requires you to be neither active nor passive. It would be best if you didn't ignore or pamper it too much – somewhere in between is much better.

Build a warm composting pile the same way you build a hot pile, but the brown and green ingredients should be equally rationed for a warm pile. Instead of every few days, turn and wet the pile every 2 to 3 weeks.

Leave the process running for 8 to 14 weeks before you attempt to apply the mixture to your garden beds or containers.

Whether you are trying hot, cold, or warm composting, never forget that activators will help both processes. Since the goal of cold composting is to take as much time as possible to produce compost, you can use natural activators instead of commercial or homemade ones. But with hot composting, it helps to use activators that will speed up the process even faster so you can have your finished humus in time for planting season.

Regardless of the method used to procure your compost, it is important to cure it before applying it to your garden. You can do this in buckets and empty containers in your house. Just make sure you put it in a place where it is sheltered from rainfall.

Curing is especially important for hot composting. First, you must allow it to mellow for no less than a month after you dig it up from the pile. That gives the microbes enough time to stabilize while the mixture's texture settles, too.

After curing, the compost becomes dark, crumbly, agreeable to the nose, and pleasurable for use in your garden. Make sure you make as much as possible because quality, organic black gold runs out faster than you can imagine.

Each method of composting has its pros and cons. You can't decide which one is best for you from the jump. The good thing is you don't need to know the answer immediately. Instead, try experimenting with each method and see which one suits you and your lifestyle better.

Also, you don't have to settle for just one method. If you wish, you can build a hot, cold, and warm pile. You can never have too much rich humus for your garden and soil amendment. More compost piles mean more compost, which invariably means more nutrients for your plants.

Chapter Six: Vermicomposting

Worms are major components in agriculture. For years, they have been used as a source of protein and enzyme for different products, from animal food to biodegradable cleansers. In addition, they have been raised as fishing bait and used to manage dairy manure and other agricultural waste products.

Vermicomposting is the art and practice of converting waste products into worm manure – a valuable nutrient-rich, beneficial soil product. It is also referred to as worm casting. In short, vermicompost is compost made from worms.

Unlike traditional composting methods like hot or cold composting, vermicomposting does not need food scraps or other organic waste materials to produce compost. The main component here is the worms.

Recently, vermicomposting has become increasingly popular amongst small and large-scale gardeners and farmers. In addition, many people in horticulture consider worm composting one of the best ways to amend and improve the soil.

The nutritional value of worm castings typically depends on what you feed to the worms – and worms, in general, feed on high-nutrient materials, such as manure and food waste. As a result, worm manure or castings offer a wide variety of essential nutrients that can help promote plant health and growth.

While much of the effects of worm castings content are still being studied, most farmers and gardeners swear by the benefits of worm manure. This is because they have witnessed the positive effects on plants first-hand. Even if the worms are fed with low-nutrient materials like paper fiber, there is still a lot to benefit from. Compared to traditional compost, vermicompost contains richer, essential nutrients such as phosphorus, nitrogen, and potassium. It also has more microbes to further plant growth.

In vermicomposting, two specific earthworms are used to produce castings: Lumbricus rubellus and Eisenia fetida. These are the most commonly used worm species for fish bait and compost production.

They are referred to by different names, including red wigglers, red worms, brandling worms, tiger worms, and manure worms. These two worm species are raised together, and difficult to differentiate from one another. But many gardeners believe they don't interbreed.

While several other worm species have been successfully bred for vermicomposting in recent years, we will focus primarily on these two species and how they produce worm manure.

Lumbricus rubellus (redworms) and Eisenia fetida (red wigglers) are excellent choices for composting because they thrive well in a compost environment than in plain soil. Plus, they are relatively easy to keep.

You won't normally find red wigglers in garden soil. On the other hand, redworms can be found near composting sites and other organic environments, such as under rotting logs. The problem here lies in identifying them.

Since you may not tell the two apart unless you are familiar with worms and their subspecies, purchasing them from a local worm supplier is much better. Or, of course, any online store that sells worms for agricultural purposes. You only need around 436 grams of worms to start a fairly big compost bin.

Worms that consume compost, vegetable waste, and organic beddings generally produce richer manure than those that consume plain soil. So, you need to create a specifically designed environment for your worms to feed on the necessary materials needed to make the optimal worm manure

Perhaps the best thing about vermicomposting bins is that they don't create a stench, which means you can keep the worms inside all year round. In addition, it's a great way to recycle your kitchen scraps even if you don't have a big backyard to compost in.

If you buy the right worms for vermicomposting and regularly feed them with necessary ingredients, you will have enough castings for your garden.

A good question you probably have in mind is, "How many worms do I need for vermicomposting?"

The number of worms in a compost bin generally depends on the number of kitchen scraps you produce. You should be able to calculate the number of worms needed in your compost by weighing the organic materials to be composted in at least one week.

Usually, the weight of the compostables relates directly to the weight of worms required for the compost bin and the surface area. Therefore, compared to traditional piles, vermicompost bins should be shallow to ensure proper worm movements.

Red wigglers work hard to decompose the components you add to the bin. They generally eat about half their weight per day. Therefore, it is best to order worms twice the amount of your weekly kitchen scrap weight. For example, if you produce one pound of scraps weekly, you will need two pounds of worms for your vermicomposting bin.

Still, the number of worms can vary greatly depending on the gardener's personal preference. While some growers like to have plenty of worms in their compost for faster results, others prefer to introduce a smaller number of worms to the bin. The two scenarios give different outcomes, which also impact the overall health and success of the compost bin.

With adequate planning and preparation of your vermicomposting bin, you can create quality organic manure at a very minimal cost.

Feeding the Worms

Worms enjoy eating, which is why they spend most of their time feeding on whatever is available. Still, they have nutritional likes and dislikes, just like humans. So, you must be specific about what you feed your worms if you want your vermicomposting endeavor to be a success.

Of the culinary likes and dislikes, fruits and veggies are some of the worms' favorite foods. They enjoy eating pumpkins, banana peels, melon rinds, leftover corn cobs, and fruit/veggie detritus. However, you shouldn't add vegetables or herbs such as onions, citrus, or garlic into the bin. The reason isn't that worms won't feed on onion or garlic, but because bulbous vegetables like garlic and onion can cause an unpleasant odor when broken down. Citrus or any other highly acidic fruit is also potentially harmful to the worms because they can kill them off in numbers. So even if you must add citrus, make sure you add the smallest amounts or leave the pulp off and only use the peel.

The ideal thing is to "go green" when feeding worms. Worms will eat almost everything that goes into your traditional compost bin, including tea leaves, plant waste, coffee grounds, and crushed eggshells. Although they may prefer green waste, worm bins should contain carbon-based materials as well.

Here are some don'ts of vermiculture feeding:

- Tomatoes and Potatoes

- Dairy products such as meat, fish, or egg

- Oily or salty food scraps

Worms eat tomatoes, but you need to ensure that the seeds have been completely broken down. Otherwise, tomatoes may sprout in your worm bin. But this is no big deal as you can just pull the tomatoes out. The same goes for potatoes. Overall, it is best to leave them out of the bin from the start.

Dairy products are strict don'ts because they tend to go rancid before even breaking down completely. Also, they can attract fruit flies and other pests to the bin. Never feed your worms with pet waste or hot manure. They can cause overheating in the bin.

Before feeding the worms, chop larger chunks of fruit and veggie scraps into tinier pieces. This will speed up the decomposition process. Depending on the bin size, a cup of food should be enough to feed the worms every two days or once per week.

Consider keeping a journal where you can keep track of how quickly the worms consume certain materials. That will enable you to adjust the varieties and amounts of meals, as well as the frequency of feeding. Note that overfeeding can lead to a stinky worm bin. Rotate the feeding areas in the bin to make sure all the worms get fed.

The best way to tell if your worms are being properly fed is to assess their conditions and increasing numbers. Taking proper care of your worms and feeding them properly is the key to getting rich compost that can benefit your soil and garden.

Kitchen Vermiculture

Kitchen vermicomposting is the practice of keeping worms in compost bins beneath your kitchen sink. If you have an indoor garden and would like to make compost for your plants, this method is the easiest. Vermicomposting indoors takes up little space. You can either build a small composting box or repurpose an old plastic bin and make a few adjustments to keep the worms in.

https://www.istockphoto.com/vector/infographic-of-vermicomposting-components-of-vermicomposter-vermicomposter-gm1301021943-393174817

- Repurpose an old plastic container or wooden box or purchase a vermicomposting kit. Note that the kit is more expensive. So, if you are composting on a budget, it is better to use the materials you already have at hand. For every pound of material you collect, one square foot of surface is enough.

- Then, you need to make beddings for the worms. Make sure the area is dark, warm, and moist with fluffy bedding. You can use straw, leaves, and shredded newspapers for the bedding. Line the box or plastic bin with five to six inches of whatever material you decide to use.

- The ideal container for worm composting should be at least 8 inches deep. That should be enough to accommodate the worms, beddings, and food scraps. If you cover the container with a tarp, punch some holes in it so that air can enter the bin.

Vermicomposting in your kitchen may not be as straightforward as hot or cold composting. However, a few trials and errors until you get it right shouldn't be a problem. Over some weeks, you will notice that the bedding and food scraps are decomposed with a clean smell.

That suggests it is time to remove the finished casting and begin the process with new worms. The composting cycle is virtually continual as long as you feed the worms and keep the bin clean.

Making a Worm Tube

Worm tubes are alternatives to traditional compost piles and bins. They are also called worm towers. A worm tube is inexpensive to make, and the process is surprisingly easy. The supplies are cheap, and you might even get them for free if you put your bartering abilities to work. It is the perfect solution for gardeners with small gardens. If you have space and would rather not use a bin, you can use a worm tube instead.

A typical worm tube comprises 5-inch tubes or pipes that are inserted into the soil. That is all you need to make a worm tube. Once you have installed the tubes in your garden bed, you can pass food scraps directly through the tube.

Worms in your garden will find the scraps and eat them, resulting in rich castings for your soil. The scraps you pass into the tubes will be turned into vermicompost.

Follow the instructions below to make a worm tube:

- Cut a metal drain or PVC pipe to 30 inches in length.

- Punch or drill multiple holes into the lower part of the pipe so the worms can easily access the scraps.

- Bury the tube about 16 inches deep into the soil.

- Use a piece of screening to wrap the top of the tube, or use a flowerpot to cover it. That will keep the pests and flies away from the tube.

The food scraps that go into the tube should be limited to non-meats such as vegetables, fruits, eggshells, and coffee grounds. At first, place a tiny amount of topsoil or compost into the tube along with the organic scraps to kick start the decomposition process.

If you don't want the worm tube to look ordinary or bland, try painting it green to blend in with the rest of your plants. Or, add some decorative elements according to your preference and style.

Harvesting Worms

How you harvest your worm castings depends on whether you are composting on a small or large scale. A large-scale farmer would need specific harvesting equipment to separate worms from castings.

Vermicomposting on a large scale involves the use of an in-vessel "continuous flow" system. The system relies on the tendency of red worms and red wigglers to surface-feed. It incorporates a harvesting mechanism at the bottom of the system, just below their active feeding area. Food and bedding are added to the surface to encourage the worms to feed upwards instead of downwards.

In smaller, more domesticated worm bins, you can harvest the castings in different ways. In general, harvesting begins when the worms have consumed food, and the bedding turns to a dark brown color, similar to the consistency of coffee grounds. If you wait longer than that, the material might become sludgy and difficult to harvest, as delayed harvesting results in anaerobic and odorous compost.

A common harvesting method is to pour the contents of the bin onto a tarp in full light. Naturally, the worms will burrow to escape the light, leaving the castings behind for you to harvest by scraping them away slowly. Make sure you occasionally pause to allow more room for the worms to burrow further. Eventually, you will have only a pile of worms left.

Another way to harvest is to add fresh bedding to one side of the bin and start feeding exclusively in the new area. After a few days or weeks, the new area should become a mass of worms. Then, using a plastic bag over your hand, you can grab the mass of worms and turn the bag inside out. This is referred to as "reverse harvesting."

The worms can then be used to start your composting bin afresh. Some eggs and worms will remain in the harvested castings, but they shouldn't be a problem if you use the compost for indoor plants. Ensure you cure the castings before applying them to outdoor plants.

Harvested worm manure can be mixed into your garden soil as soon as you've collected it. That way, it has the best effect on your houseplants. If you plan to store or use it for outdoor plants, cure it in an aerobic environment first. Curing means allowing it to dry to eliminate the possibility of new species developing and preventing mold from forming.

Vermicompost Tea

The conventional way of applying compost to plants is to mix it into the soil, and vermicompost tea is a liquid alternative to solid compost. Also referred to as worm casting tea, you can produce it when you sieve and steep some of your vermicompost into ordinary water, the same way you would tea leaves.

The result is all-natural liquid manure that you can dilute and use to water your indoor or outdoor plants. You can make vermicompost tea for plants in a few ways. The most straightforward is to scoop some handfuls of compost from your bin and pour it into a five-gallon bucket filled with water. Then, you let the mixture soak overnight.

By morning, the water should have turned to a mild brown color. After this, you can steep the liquid for as long as you need. The vermicompost tea is easy to apply to plants. Just dilute the brown liquid in a 1:3 tea to water ratio, after which you can use it to water your plants.

Note that you can't leave the tea for longer than 48 hours before application. Otherwise, it will go bad. You can use an old stocking or tee shirt as a tea bag for steeping to make the liquid neater.

Chapter Seven: Working with Containers

Container gardening is a thing, which means container composting must be a thing too. The benefits of making your compost are too good to pass up simply for living in an apartment or not having enough space to build a pile. That is why it is possible to make compost in containers.

If you have a variety of pots sitting around and don't have enough space for a backyard pile or compost bin, you can use those pots to good use. It's quite easy to make a compost or worm bin from plastic storage containers.

Container composting is the perfect solution for gardeners with space at a premium or gardeners who just want a little black gold to boost the growth of their flowers and vegetables. The point is that you don't need a big yard or garden to make compost.

There are various types of containers you can use indoors to make compost. For example, small bins can fit under the kitchen sink or cabinet, a tiny space in the pantry, or any other place where you have space.

You can use the following items as containers for indoor composting:

- Wooden boxes

- Bucket or pail

- Rubbermaid containers

- Tumbler

Composting tumblers are quite popular among gardeners, not minding the price. Some rotate on an elevated base, while some are rolled along on the ground. Some rotate around an axle, and some need cranking with a handle.

These types of tumblers produce compost easily and, in less time, than a traditional bin. Should you be wondering whether to get a tumbler or not, let's examine the qualities and features.

In 2011, a gardening magazine in the United Kingdom conducted a test with composting tumblers and traditional bins. The test compared turning well-filled tumblers thrice per week and turning a basic compost pile of the same size once per week. To many people's surprise, they found that tumblers took a month longer than traditional heaps to produce finished organic compost.

The result of that short test suggests that while tumblers make turning easy, you might also stick to a standard compost pile or bin if you want to compost more quickly.

Of course, not everyone turns out compost every week. Some don't mind waiting as long as 14 weeks to access usable compost. A tumbler is great if you want to compost in containers. But before you get one, put the following into consideration:

- The tumbler should be easy to turn. Otherwise, there is no point.

- Large tumblers compost more efficiently than smaller ones.

• To produce compost within three weeks, you have to fill up the tumbler in one go. Don't add bulk materials once the process is underway – you might have to wait longer for finished humus.

• Compost tumblers work best during the summer. However, unless you insulate them fully, the cold winter weather can stop them from fully powering and heating up.

Undoubtedly, there is a distinctive difference between compost made in a tumbler and a traditional heap. This difference is inevitable for a few reasons. First, organic scraps in a tumbler are broken down mostly by bacteria and fungi.

You can add worms to the tumbler, but they will die once the temperature becomes too high. That eliminates all the productive work worms put in a standard heap or bin.

Other than the increased turning workout, there are several other reasons to consider composting in a tumbler.

• Tumblers are great if you have a rat or raccoon problem in your yard. The right tumbler proffers an immediate solution to vermin issues. In addition, the metallic material and the elevated position mean you don't need huge air gaps to aerate your pile.

• You can compost ordinarily forbidden foods in a tumbler. For example, fish, fat, meat, oil, cheese, and many others can be conveniently included in a tumbler with no fear of pests. Also, the high temperature allows them to decompose in a short time.

• If you struggle with back or spine problems, you can't turn compost too often. That's why choosing your equipment based on your needs is important. For example, please don't get a tumbler that requires pushing it along the ground. The best type for you, in this case, is the one that is turned via the handle and geared cogs.

• Tumblers are perfect for gardeners with tons and tons of composting materials in the yard. However, too much grass and leaf clippings can lead to anaerobic decomposition. Since a tumbler generates air so readily, it can be used to compost plenty amounts of grass clippings without the fear of compaction.

- A tumbler is perfect if you don't have space for a traditional pile.

- You can make compost in as little as three weeks with a tumbler. So, if your objective is ultra-fast output, you are better off getting a tumbler.

The overall conclusion is that tumbler composters are good for someone with limited space. They also make organic materials decompose more quickly, which means they produce usable compost in a short period. Although compact, they need more room than all the other mentions listed above. One place you can put them is on your deck or patio.

The process of making an indoor compost container is easy, and you can set yours up in less than an hour with just your container, a knife, or a drill.

- 18-gallon plastic container

- One knife or drill

- Two lids for the plastic container

You can either purchase a basic plastic storage container from a Home or Office Depot around you or just about any multi-purpose store you find. However, if you want to live modestly and spend as little money as possible, you can pick up a storage container at any garage sale for an incredibly low price.

If you don't want to spend money at all, look into your garage, and you might find a container that is just sitting there, waiting for you to pick it up for composting. The purpose of the knife or drill is to make holes in the plastic to ensure proper aeration and air circulation.

Suppose you have neither knife nor drill, and you don't want to spend money on a new one; get creative and use a hammer and nail or screwdriver to drill the holes.

Compost needs lots of air circulation, so you have to punch as many holes as possible in the container. Ensure the holes are tiny enough to let air in but not too big to let compost ooze out. Drill the holes along the container sides, the base, and on the lid. They should be 2 inches apart.

To prevent possible oozing, line the interior of the plastic container with a hardware cloth or wire mesh. The second lid should go to the bottom of the pot to collect whatever oozes out of it. That will prevent the compost area from becoming messy, no matter where you put it.

One of the beauties of container composting is that you can place your container in any part of your home. Thanks to their size, containers rarely take up much room. Still, the best place to put it is near your kitchen door, where you can easily toss scraps inside after every meal.

You can also place it closer to your garden so you can toss in plants during your de-weeding process. Some gardeners place their compost containers in the garage, but you shouldn't do that if you want to avoid a buildup of stinky odors in your garage after a few weeks of composting.

Everything that goes in a traditional pile goes in a compost container. However, you have to ensure they are as finely chopped as possible. Only fill your pot with small pieces of organic matter that will break down easily once microbial activity starts. Chop and dice the fruits and veggies, crush the eggshells, and shred the leaves with your leaf shredder or lawnmower.

In a compost container, smaller is always better for both the gardener and the decomposing organisms. Refer back to more information on the materials you can add to your container.

Some gardeners sprinkle a little dirt into their compost container from time to time. You don't have to do this, but it is helpful to an extent. As you add more items into the pot, ensure the compost remains damp to prevent that unpleasant stench we mentioned throughout the previous chapters.

If the compost becomes too wet at any point, add more shredded paper or leaves to the mix to absorb the moisture. Conversely, you should add a little water to the pot if the compost becomes too dry.

Maintaining the container is simple – just give it a little shake every one or two days to keep the inside aerated. Since the size of the container pile would probably be small, you don't need to turn the compost.

To aid the process, you can introduce worms to the pile. They will do the job in half the time, and you won't need to gather more items for them to feed on. They will happily feed on the organic waste already available in the pot.

Take a piece of newspaper, place it on the ground in your backyard and sprinkle a little water. Make sure to do so directly on the dirt. Check back the next morning, and you should find a writhing mass of feeding worms on the newspaper. Pack them up and incorporate them into the compost container. It's as simple as that.

How to Store Scraps for Your Compost Container

Once you start composting in containers, you need to have a regular supply of scraps to add more to your pile. Unless you are willing to rush to the container every time you peel a banana or de-weed your garden, you need a storage system for the scraps. And the system has to be one where they remain compostable until you are ready to add them to the container.

Here are some of the ways to store scraps:

• **Compost Crock:** If you want to store scraps on your countertop, you need to consider aesthetics. You need something more attractive than a plain plastic bucket to prevent disrupting your kitchen's whole look. A compost crock may be the ideal solution for this. It is usually made of ceramic or stainless steel and won't look out of place on a countertop. More importantly, crocks are preinstalled with charcoal filters to prevent the smell of the scraps from filtering out and ruining your kitchen. The average crock costs $20 to $60, so they aren't necessarily cheap.

• **Coffee Can:** If you don't produce too much kitchen waste, you just need a small container like a coffee can to store the scraps. A coffee can, maybe steel or pure plastic – either works fine. Make sure to save the lid, and you will have yourself a convenient container for organic scraps. You can keep the can in the fridge to regulate the smell and keep the odor from permeating the environment. This is especially important if you plan to empty and refill the container every day.

• **Compost Bucket or Pail:** Chapter Two mentioned compost pails as one of the best tools to buy before you begin composting. This remains true whether you are composting in a garden or container. A bucket or pail is a perfect solution if you have a place in your pantry or cabinet to keep the food scraps. A pail is made of plastic or steel. Plastic pails are generally less expensive than steel ones. Some of the metal pails have installed filters similar to the ones in compost crocks. The plastic ones have air-tight lids to prevent the smell of scraps from escaping into the environment. Prices range between $10 and $50, depending on whether you are getting a plastic or steel pail.

• **Repurposed Plastic Paint or Detergent Bucket:** If you regularly buy bulk-sized paint or detergent, the bucket can be repurposed to store scraps. Wash the container thoroughly to get all chemicals out, keep the lids, and start using it to store food scraps. Since the buckets are quite large, you can use one to save plenty of scraps before emptying them into the composting container. The only problem is that odor can build up in the container, but this is solvable by sprinkling some Bokashi mix onto the pile every time you add new scraps.

• **Plastic Bags**: Kitchen scraps for your composting container can be stored and refrigerated until you need them. Alternatively, you can even freeze the collected scraps if you don't need to add new scraps to your pot yet. The good thing about refrigerating them is that there won't be any odors. Plus, scraps break down faster when they have gone through freezing and thawing.

It is okay to experiment a few times till you find the container system that works for you. Once you have decided on a specific system, you can start using the storage supply whenever you need new scraps for your composting container.

Maintaining a container is the easiest thing to do. The compost in your bin or container will thrive with the right mix of scraps and dry materials. Although you don't need to turn the container, it doesn't hurt to do that periodically. That will help the compost develop even faster, especially with the presence of worms.

There is no schedule to follow in turning and aerating the compost. However, you shouldn't do it every day as this can disrupt the microbial activities going on, which is quite easy to do in a fairly fun-sized container.

Don't forget to add natural activators to your container as the process progresses. A commercial activator may not be necessary since the size of the pot will make decomposition happen more quickly.

As you would in a bin or the ground, spritz the container with water to keep the content damp and nice.

Chapter Eight: Working without Containers

Many people think that composting can only happen in a bin or container. The fact is you can choose to compost without any container if that is what you want. Composting without containers can be done in two ways: below ground or above ground.

Composting above ground is done in a freestanding pile, while below ground is referred to as trench composting because it involves digging holes into the ground. Freestanding piles are heaps of organic waste gathered and piled up with no enclosure to corral them.

There are many reasons why you should consider working without containers or bins. First, the expenses are quite minimal, compared to composting in bins or containers. There is nothing cheaper than gathering a pile of grass clippings and leaves and making a compost pile directly below or above the ground.

To decide on which no-container option is best for you, just think of your available space. For example, if you have lots of space and elbow room, freestanding composting piles are great. But make sure the available space is in a location where your neighbors don't have to deal with the not-so-appealing sight of your pile.

If you have plenty of backyard space and lots of organic material to decompose, you can build larger freestanding piles called windrows.

However, if the soil in your home is convenient to dig through, trench composting below the ground is an excellent option. Trench composting is also a great way to put your kitchen scraps to work without attracting pests or flies.

Both trench and freestanding composting are excellent options if you want to compost in future planting areas. This is one thing you can try if you haven't started gardening yet, or if you have plans to change your gardening site.

Composting in that designated area will improve the quality and health of the soil there before you finally start planting.

The problem with no-bin composting is that the pile often looks messy, especially when you don't clean and maintain it well. Regardless of how hard you try to tidy a freestanding pile, you can't completely keep pests away. Raccoons, rodents, dogs, badgers, and other wildlife will always find their way there in search of something to feed on.

If the ground in your home is rocky and difficult to dig up, do not try trench composting. Otherwise, you'd have to deal with the struggles of digging up a new hole every day. And even when you do manage to dig a spot, you might end up without usable compost due to the incompatibility of the soil.

The instructions in chapter three can be followed to build a freestanding pile. The difference is that you don't use a box or bin because the pile is built directly in the ground. Trench composting, on the other hand, requires a little more dive-in.

Trench Composting

The idea of trench composting is that gardeners can compost by digging holes in the ground and burying organic matter, which safely decomposes and feeds the plants around that area.

Trench composting is done strategically. In short, you can select spots where to put your composting holes so that your outdoor plants can benefit from the underground compost through their roots.

You can follow different trench composting techniques to create quality, odor-free compost right in your garden, where you need it the most, without having to turn or maintain it. Instead, just dig the hole, bury the organic materials, and leave it to decompose naturally while your plants automatically benefit.

The whole process might seem straightforward, but there would not be much to explain if it was just about digging holes and burying food scraps. If you want to keep it simple, of course, that alone is enough.

Simply dig a hole that is at least a foot deep and wide, stuff it with all sorts of compostable materials and add the dirt back on top. Do this in several spots across your garden until you've successfully covered the whole area. That's it – you are done making your trench compost.

However, a little more strategy is required if you want to get the best out of the compost you make. Naturally, gardeners make compost to feed it to their plants to improve their growth and health.

What trench composting offers is a way for you to make compost in the exact place where it is needed so that your whole garden can feast on its nutrients and grow. An important detail to always have at the back of your mind is that the plants shouldn't be directly above the compost spot.

If your roots grow into nothing but a mass of rotting matter, it will probably cause a few problems, such as root rot. Consequently, you can dig a hole or a trench in an area, fill it with organic material, and cover it up with soil. Then, you can cultivate your plants adjacent to the composting area.

The nutrients will circulate in the soil, meaning that your plants will reap the reward of composting without suffering root rot or any potentially damaging problem.

A good way to achieve this is to do this in a garden bed and cycle through a few compost trenches surrounded by healthy plant life. By the time you cycle back around, you will be digging up rich black gold.

Another method is to build a vertical composting garden specifically designed for annual crops. This goes beyond the usual conventional rows of plants. In a vertical garden, the rows come in sets of three. The first is a normal path for walking, so you don't trample the plants. The second is a suppressed composting trench that is filled gradually with biodegradable materials. And finally, the last is the usual planting row.

Each row assumes a new role every time you fill up the trench: the walking path becomes the new trench, the old compost becomes the planting row, and the planting row becomes the walking path. As you keep rotating, the soil in your gardener becomes richer with each season.

The technique above is perfect for you if your neighborhood does not allow composting bins. It is also a great way to convert your yard space to an edible garden gradually. Just add a new garden bed each time you dig a new compost trench or hole.

Soon, all the scrap from your kitchen will be filling your fridge and kitchen with fresh, new produce instead of wasting away in garbage dumps.

To speed up the decomposition process in trenches, always sprinkle a few handfuls of blood meal atop the organic waste before burying it with soil. Also, water deep in the hole before covering it up.

You might need to wait at least six weeks for the organic materials to start decomposing. After then, you can plant something adjacent to the trench. For a larger trench, fill the materials evenly or dig in deeper with your pitchfork or shovel.

Chapter Nine: Keeping Pests Out

It's impossible to keep pests away from a compost pile completely, but their presence can be greatly reduced. A question many often ask is, "Should there be bugs in my compost pile?" As long as you are composting, you are bound to have bugs. If your compost pile is not properly constructed, it may become overrun with insects.

Different insects visit compost piles, with the most common ones being:

> • **Houseflies:** Common houseflies are always found around decaying matter because they enjoy feasting on the tasty treat. They generally prefer manure and rotting waste, but you will find them in composted materials such as lawn clippings and others.

> • **Stable Flies:** Like houseflies, stable flies have a sharp needle-like beak protruding from their heads. They have a knack for laying eggs in piles of manure mixed with straw, grass clippings, and wet straw.

• **Green June Beetles:** These are metallic green beetles that are about one to two inches long. They can be mostly found laying eggs in rotting organic matter.

In general, it is not a bad thing to have bugs in one's compost. However, they can get out of hand if you don't manage them properly. The best way to regulate their presence in your pile is to increase the carbon content and sprinkle a few handfuls of bone meal to keep the heap damp. Spraying around the compost area with an orange-scented spray may also help to reduce the fly population.

Depending on your residential area, rodents and raccoons are some other pests you are likely to have a problem with. Of course, domestic animals like dogs aren't exempted from the list of potential intruders either. After all, organic compost is an attractive source of food and shelter for many animals. So, it's important to learn how to keep those animals out.

If you manage your pile well by turning and aerating it as frequently as required, animals shouldn't find your compost that attractive. Instead, stick to the recommended brown to green ratio to reduce the number of food scraps that could invite pests to the pile.

Be sure to leave meat or any other dairy product off the pile. Do not even put leftovers of cheese, oil, or seasoning into the compost, as these are all magnets for rodents and raccoons. Also, place your bin away from any location that is a natural food source for animals. Examples include pet food bowls, bird feeders, and berry trees.

Sometimes, keeping animals out of a compost pile is as simple as using a specific compost bin system to keep them away. While many people have success with open composting systems, they are generally more difficult to maintain than enclosed ones when making compost. On the other hand, a closed bin system can help keep pests at bay. Although most animals, especially raccoons and rodents, often dig under the bin, a closed system is harder for animals to penetrate.

Now that you know the general ways to keep pests from composts, let's dig into the specifics.

How to Protect Your Compost from Rats and Mice

The first place rats run to for warmth and food during cold climate is the nearest compost pile. Where better than a place with plenty of food scraps to feed on and a little bit of heat to keep the body warm?

It is normal to get rats in your compost pile, but you absolutely cannot allow them to thrive there. Rats are linked to everything from hantavirus to Lyme disease. Many of the diseases they transmit are present in their feces. There is nothing to describe the feeling of disgust you feel as a gardener when you find the tiny mice feces all over your pile or kitchen tabletop.

Keeping mice away from the inside of your home is an easy feat. But keeping them out of your compost pile is an entirely different ballgame! Mice in a compost pile during the winter months are quite problematic.

During summer, when you have the option of turning and aerating your pile frequently, mice and rats only come there to glean food. However, once it's winter, they swarm available compost piles because they have everything rats and mice need to survive the harsh winter.

Not only does a pile offer quality insulation against the cold weather, but it also provides an environment to self-generate heat. In addition, compost heaps are drier during winter when they aren't frequently watered and turned, making them even more inviting to critters. So, for the rodents, a compost pile is a blessing.

Sealing up your compost heap is one way to keep rodents out, but it often turns out to be a frustrating endeavor. The little critters end up crawling back in by digging tiny gaps that are no bigger than a single penny. They can also chew through any screen or tarp you place at the top or bottom of the pile with their sharp teeth.

Just when you think you have successfully sealed up the heap with screens to prevent them from burrowing in, they surprise you by simply crawling inside through the side of the frame. You'd be surprised at how resourceful and creative they can be when it comes to invading an available compost pile.

An excellent solution to this problem is to put your pile in a barrel elevated off the ground. And that means using a compost tumbler or getting a commercial compost bin that can keep the rodents out.

Some gardeners say they keep rodents away from large, open compost piles by making the piles less inviting. But if that doesn't work, you might need to set traps. Before you start setting traps, here are some tips that could work:

• When it's fall and mice are moving into your pile, soak it well. Rats and mice don't like moist bedding conditions. Use some warm snaps to make the pile even wetter and unattractive to rodents.

• Rodents don't like to be disturbed once they've settled in a pile. So again, take advantage of warm snaps to turn your pile as much as you can.

• Do not add food scraps to the pile during the winter months. Instead, use a vermicompost bin or bokashi bucket to convert your food scraps into a quality soil amendment.

• Cover the heap with a lid or tarp. Although this doesn't necessarily keep the rodents from getting inside the compost, it reduces air circulation, keeping mice away during the winter months.

If you decide to set traps, be as careful as possible. When mice infest your heap, you have to take some precautionary measures – setting traps is one of those measures to take. No matter the kind of trap you use, always wear gloves to prevent direct contact with the mouse or its fecal matter.

It is also good to wear a breathing mask to avoid breathing in the fecal dust around the environment. Finally, once you catch mice, dispose of them properly, and if you can, humanely.

The steps below are specifically for keeping rats away but can also work for mice:

1. Use your wooden, open-slatted compost bin for garden waste only. For vegetable scraps and other kitchen waste, use a commercial plastic container with a rat-proof base. If your compost bin is **DIY**, then put it on mesh wire. Rats can gnaw through 15mm gaps in mesh wire, so you need to make sure the holes in your mesh are tinier than that. Also, it should be heavy-duty. Do not use chicken wire since it isn't as strong as these rodents' teeth.

2. Set the bin squarely to leave no gap between the lid and the sides. That makes it considerably more difficult for rats to chew their way in. Be careful not to leave any edge for them to nibble on.

3. Rats like to keep to edges and passages because they are secretive pests. Therefore, keep your compost out in the open as much as possible. This means keeping it away from the sides of the building and other corners where rats can hide. The lack of proper cover will discourage them from setting up a home.

4. Put the bin in a location you pass by regularly and do a quick rat-a-tat on the side of the bin every time you pass. That is another way to discourage them from making your compost pile their home.

Try looking around your garden from a rat's perspective. Then, try to determine how likely they are to set up home in your pile even after you've followed the instructions above.

How to Get Rid of Raccoons

Raccoons are another pest you might have to deal with once you start your pile. They are mischievous and can cause more havoc than any other pest. It's important to learn how to keep them away from your compost pile. If you let them linger around your heap, they will soon get into your garden. Fortunately, the task of getting rid of raccoons or keeping them away from your pile is not necessarily trying.

Eliminating raccoons from your yard can be as easy as tidying up the area or as complicated as setting traps. You can also use deterrents or prevent them from getting into your garden through fencing. While their activities usually happen in the garden, it's not uncommon to find them in garbage cans and around pets' food.

Therefore, the first step is to seal the lids of your trashcans tight, so these pests can't open them. Also, if you have any pets, keep their food away at night since raccoons are most active at nighttime.

You may not always witness their visit in person, but raccoons tend to leave behind signs of their visit. This may not be noticeable in a compost pile, but you can tell when they've been in a garden. They leave droppings, tracks and cause crop damage. If you spot any of these signs, chances are the raccoons have been in your compost pile too.

Various techniques can be used to scare these pests away – some of which include using flashlights, radio, pie pans, or scarecrows. These are all temporary solutions, though, because it does not take long for the animals to get used to them.

Nevertheless, there are more proactive preventive measures. For instance, raccoons like to hide in brush piles, hollow trees, and logs, etc. So, cleaning up those areas can help keep them away from your yard at large. You should also clear out any debris and overgrown shrubbery around. Close open compost piles with screens and prune the overhanging trees to prevent the pests from climbing into your home via the rooftops.

Fencing is your best bet for eliminating raccoons from your composting area. However, since they are skilled diggers and climbers, it is not enough to set up ordinary fencing - raccoon-proof fencing needs a little bit of electricity.

You need one or two strands of electric fencing material that are about 8 inches from the ground and away from the fence. You should also consider burying the fencing 5 to 6 inches deep with a foot out to stop them from digging their way underneath.

Alternatively, you can install two strands of electric fence around your composting perimeter. The bottom strand should be elevated at least 6 inches off the ground. Then, you can easily turn the electricity on and off at will. Nighttime is the best time to leave it on, but you can during the day if you wish.

If the other methods don't keep them out, and you decide on trapping the raccoons, leave that to a professional! Do not attempt to set up the trap yourself unless you are confident you know what you are doing.

To trap raccoons, use a heavy, cage-type gauge trap that is at least 10x12x32 inches. You can add anything from fresh fruits to fish-flavored pet food as bait for the trap. If you capture any raccoon, make sure you find out the appropriate areas to relocate it to in your region.

Note that it may be illegal to capture and release raccoons into federal land and parks. So, make sure you ask one of your local representatives about safe and lawful relocation.

Predator Urine as a Pest Deterrent

Of all pests that could swarm your pile, mammals are the ones likely to cause the most damage. So, it is crucial to keep them away from the vicinity. One of the most effective strategies to ward them off your compost heap and yard is to use a pest deterrent.

Predator urine is the most common deterrent for mammals. It is categorized as an olfactory repellent, meaning it targets a pest's sense of smell. Fox and coyote urine are the most commonly used repellent for smaller mammals like dogs, but other types of animal urines are available, too.

Gardeners have mixed reviews about predator urine. Fox urine is said to work best for deterring smaller mammals like cats, squirrels, rabbits, etc. Coyote urine repels larger predators like deer and works against raccoons and other smaller mammals such as woodchucks, skunks, etc.

Although not a foolproof solution, predator urine as a deterrent works pretty well. The only problem is that the pests might eventually become habituated to the scent of the urine and return to the compost.

The solution to this is to swap out the repellent once a month. Another problem is olfactory repellents are unlikely to stop animals that are determined and hungry enough. Generally, repellents are a much better choice for keeping pests out of a composting area or garden than traps and poisons.

Plus, they are less expensive than installing an electric fence or a netting system. Still, setting up physical barriers is more reliable than using predator urine to deter pests.

Before picking a control method, it helps to know the exact kinds of pests getting into your compost pile. For example, since you are more likely to get raccoons and rodents in your pile, you can use a fox and coyote urine mix.

To determine the kinds of mammals getting in your compost or yard, examine the type of damage, the time it occurred, and the targeted area.

Note that coyote urine may attract dogs or coyotes around the area, so it may be best to use fox urine. Reapply the urine products after any rain or weekly, depending on the instructions on the product.

To increase the potency, consider buying multiple types of pest repellent. If you don't want to use predator urine as a pest deterrent, try other methods like fencing or netting.

Chapter Ten: Tips on How to Best Use Your Compost

Seasoned composters know when compost is matured and ready for use, owing to their experience. However, as a beginner, you need some pointers and directions. As you compost more and more, thereby gaining more experience, you won't be needing these tips to know when compost is finished.

Several variables affect the timing of mature compost. For example, the size of the organic materials used in a pile, the frequency of turning, moisture level, the temperature in the pile, and the brown to green ratio are all factors that determine how long it takes for compost to become ready.

It can take anywhere from 1 to 12 months for compost to finally become a mature product, factoring in the elements above and the intended usage of the product. For instance, if you plan to apply compost as a top dressing, it takes very little time.

Finished compost, also referred to as humus, is intended for use as a soil amendment and growing medium. Therefore, it needs to get to a level where you are certain that it's finished. Using unfinished compost can negatively affect your plant's health. Never mix immature compost into your soil before it reaches the final humus stage.

As previously explained, finished humus has a dark and crumbly texture, accompanied by an earthly smell. By the time compost is ready, the pile size would have reduced by half, and there should be no visible organic material. If you use the hot composting method, there shouldn't be much heat left.

Understandably, these tips may not be enough to ascertain when compost is ready for use. Thankfully, there are scientific ways of testing compost maturity. However, these methods can take some time.

The fastest method involves digging up some compost from your pile, putting it inside two containers, and then sprinkling some radish seeds on it. If at least 75 percent of the seeds sprout and germinate into radishes, you have mature compost for your garden. Radishes germinate and develop quite quickly, which is why they are recommended for this test.

Other more complicated methods are used in formal settings, meaning you can't try them at home. Unfinished compost contains phytotoxin, which can stop seeds from germinating or even kill the sprouts as soon as they grow, making it a counterproductive tool.

So, if you try the radish test and it doesn't sprout or dies off soon after sprouting, it could mean that the phytotoxin levels are still significant enough to cause damage. But if you attain an acceptable germination rate, that means your organic compost is ready and safe to use in your garden.

Checking your soil PH levels is a common practice in gardening. The point of the test is to determine the acidity level of the soil to ensure that it's safe for growing your crops. Just as you would check the soil PH levels, it helps to check your compost PH range.

First, the result you get will inform you about the current PH and let you know if you should change the pile. In short, you will know whether to lower the compost PH or increase it.

Mature compost that is ready for use always has a PH range between 6 and 8. As the pile decays, the PH changes, meaning that the range will vary at different stages of the process. Most plants need a neutral PH of around 7 to thrive, but some enjoy a more acidic PH.

And that is where you understand the importance of checking the PH. Depending on the plants in your garden, you can finetune the compost to make it more or less acidic or alkaline.

During different composting stages, you will notice that the temperature in the pile fluctuates. As the temp varies, so does the PH. As a result, the PH level might be different in certain parts of the compost heap.

Therefore, when testing the PH level of your compost, ensure you extract the compost from several areas of the pile. You can use a soil test kit to measure the PH. There are instructions to follow in the packet. If you have a pile that is damp but not muddy, use a PH indicator strip instead. An electric soil meter is also effective for reading the compost PH range.

The soil kit will tell you how acidic or alkaline the compost is, but what if you need a more acidic compost to amend your soil and its alkaline nature? The thing with compost is that it is capable of balancing soil PH.

What that means is, if your soil is acidic, finished compost can raise the PH level naturally. However, it can also lower the PH in soil that is too alkaline.

That being said, it's sometimes better to decrease compost PH before it becomes ready for use. The best way to achieve this is to incorporate more acidic materials into compost as it decomposes. Oak leaves and pine needles are great examples of acidic materials. Ericaceous compost is the kind of compost made specifically for acid-loving plants. You may also lower compost PH after it is finished and ready to use. When you mix it into the soil, simply add an amendment like aluminum sulfate.

You can create a highly acidic compost by encouraging more anaerobic bacteria into your compost pile. Normally, composting is meant to be aerobic, meaning that decomposition is spearheaded by organisms that require oxygen – that is why you turn the compost.

If you deprive the pile of oxygen, anaerobic bacteria take charge of decomposition. Composting in trenches, bags, or with garbage can lead to anaerobic composting. Note that the result of this is highly acidic compost.

Anaerobic compost has a PH that is too high for most plants. In this case, you should expose it to air for at least a month to neutralize the PH level.

Regularly turning and aerating a compost pile is the quickest way to improve airflow and encourage aerobic bacteria. It is also the most effective way to reduce acidity in your compost. You can also use lime to increase the alkalinity of your pile but only do so after the compost is ready. Do not add it directly to the process as that can trigger the release of ammonium nitrogen gas.

In general, you may not need to amend the PH of your compost since it already has the natural ability to balance the PH levels in the soil. So, only amend your compost PH if you find it necessary.

Compost can be used in different ways. If you've never applied compost in your garden or anywhere else, you may need some pointers on how to use your organic compost. This can be especially tricky if you have a big yard or outdoor garden. The good thing is there are many beneficial things you can do with that organic compost.

There is a reason why compost is called "black gold." It adds rich nutrients to ordinary soil to help crops grow healthier and more productively. If you want healthy soil to build fertility in your garden, compost is an excellent idea.

Mixing your soil with organic compost improves its structure, allowing it to retain more moisture and nutrients. Compared to commercial fertilizers, compost improves soil quality at a steady and permanent pace. It also encourages microbial activities in the soil, improving its nutrient uptake.

Below are some of the basic ways to apply compost and use your home-made black gold:

- **Soil Amendment:** Mixing compost into the soil in garden beds or containers before planting seeds lightens and aerates the soil. Most importantly, it adds essential nutrients to it.

- **Mulch:** You can use compost as mulch around the plants in your garden beds. Like any mulch type, the compost retains moisture and warmth in the soil. It also provides the plants with much-needed extra nutrients. Add a layer of compost that is 2 to 3 inches thick around the base of the plants in your garden. Lay it out to about 1ft from the base.

- **Fertilize:** Compost can also serve as fertilizer for your lawn. First, add one or two-inch layers of compost to your grass instead of commercial fertilizer. Then, rake the humus in and leave it to work its magic deep down into the roots.

- **Compost Tea:** If you want a liquid fertilizer for your plants, you can make compost tea using the instructions in chapter six. Spray the liquid on your plants to boost their growth.

If you don't have a garden or lawn, you can still use compost for your potted indoor plants. Some of the ways you can use compost include:

- Mix basic soil with compost to make potting soil for your container plants.

• Amend your ordinary potting soil with compost for better and healthier growth.

• Make compost tea to fertilize your container and indoor plants.

• Find a curbside compost collection in your local area and donate the organic compost to the community.

It's one thing to know how to apply compost to your garden, lawn, or container plants. Knowing the quantity to use is another thing entirely. How can you tell how much compost is enough for your plants? What if you use too much compost?

The appropriate quantity of compost for plants depends on specific factors. As good as compost is for your garden soil, you must be moderate in its use. You should add 1-3 inches of compost to your vegetable garden beds or containers as a rule of thumb. It should be thoroughly blended into the soil. Unfortunately, that isn't always the case.

Sometimes, the amount of compost you add to your garden depends on what you hope to accomplish with it. For example, if your goal is to improve the nutrients level in your soil, the first step to take is doing a soil test to ascertain which nutrients the soil needs, if any.

You should also run a nutrient check on the compost since nutrient levels vary based on the type of composted detritus. For example, a pile that contained lots of lawn clippings will have less nitrogen than the one with more eggshells and fruit peels.

If your goal is to improve your soil structure with compost, examine the texture of your current soil. If it has a sandy texture, adding compost would be an excellent choice. The compost will enhance the texture and allow the soil to retain more moisture, even with its sandiness. It will also develop the nutrient supply.

Clay soils tend to have poor drainage, so if your garden soil is clay, you can have too much compost. Don't use compost with clay soil, as that can worsen the drainage issue. That happens for the same reason it helps with moisture retention.

One common question new gardeners often ask is, "Can compost expire or get old?" This is a good question because the answer gives an insight into what to do if your compost ever becomes too old.

Open compost heaps are built in a location out of everybody's way, so it's quite easy to forget about them. Don't be surprised if you forget your pile. Neglect makes a pile turn plain, dry, and moldy. Fortunately, it is possible to revitalize old compost. If you ever need to do that, this information will be helpful.

Neglected compost often fails to decompose while losing nutrients. It takes a bit of effort to reawaken an old pile, but it's nothing you can't do. After revitalization, you get fairly good humus for your plants.

During the winter season, most piles often look dead due to reduced heat and decreased microbial activity. However, they aren't necessarily dead. An old or dead pile is immediately recognizable by the dry and grayish appearance and the absence of insects such as pill bugs and earthworms.

There are several methods for reviving old compost. Still, these methods may not make the compost rich enough to start seeding or propagate. With careful management, though, it will still make a good addition to your soil and garden beds. Even if the hummus is inert, its organic features can help aerate and improve the texture of heavy soils.

Here are some ways to bring a pile back to life:

- Add in plenty of nitrogen sources to kickstart the process.
- Keep the brown materials slightly lower than the greens.
- Turn the pile three times a week and keep it mildly moist but not muddy.

In a short period, there should be visible differences in the appearance of the pile. For example, decomposing organisms should reappear to help break down the organic materials. In a sunny spot, the pile should be teeming with organic life and microbial activity. To enhance the process even more, add tons of worms to help the materials decompose faster.

If you would rather not go through all that trouble, you can still use the neglected compost as long as it isn't moldy. If moldy, dry it off in the sun for a week to kill off the mold spores.

You can energize non-moldy compost with fertilizer. Follow a time-release formula and add some gritty materials if it is clumpy. You may need to break down the larger chunks and clumps manually.

Alternatively, dig a trench and bury the compost in your garden. Over time, microbes in the soil will break it down and revitalize it to an extent. It may not have lots of nutrients, but it will improve soil composition and help, even if it's on a minimal scale.

How to Store Compost

Space is one of the major considerations in storing compost. It's simply unattractive to leave compost on the ground, plus it needs plenty of garden space which you may not have like many home gardeners.

You can leave the compost in its bin and keep it moist and aerated. But if you, like many gardeners, set up a system that gives you a consistent batch of finished compost, you need to find other ways to store it. In this case, it can be stored in plastic bags and garbage cans. Just get a few of these and store the compost in them.

Another way to store compost is in the form of compost tea, easily one of the best ways to apply compost to an organic garden. Not only does compost tea fertilize the soil, but it can also protect plants from insects and pests.

Compost tea is storable for up to five days in sealed containers. The container should be lightproof. To store it longer, keep it aerated with an aquarium pump or bubbler stone. Storing compost tea for future use ensures you have a supply of beneficial microbes to improve your plants' growth and health.

Ideally, you should always use your compost as soon as possible. The longer you store it, the more likely it is to lose nutrients.

Chapter Eleven: Compost Maintenance Tips

Maintaining compost can be a strenuous task. Nonetheless, it is non-negotiable. Many gardeners dread cleaning out their compost piles and bins. Dedicating a bin to storing garden waste and rotting food can create a foul-smelling mess, especially in summer.

You need to clean the pile regularly to avoid pests and prevent odors from permeating your environment. If you leave it uncleaned for too long, you might need a gas mask to clean up. As you move out finished compost and add new materials to your heap, make sure you are cleaning around the area as well.

If you have a small compost bin for collecting kitchen scraps, place it in the freezer to manage the sanitary conditions and prevent odors as much as possible. You should wash the bin regularly the same way you do your dishes.

To wash the compost bin, you need a hose and natural cleaners. Don't use soap because it can damage the local ecosystem. Instead, make a cleaning mixture from lemon, vinegar, and baking soda to deodorize and sanitize the container. Lining your bin with newspaper and sprinkling it with baking soda is one way to ensure it stays clean for longer periods. Also, use compostable bags to store scraps.

Since you will be using most of your compost, you don't need to do a full cleaning too often. Instead, you need to focus on tidying the area whenever you scoop finished compost from the pile. Once a year, you should remove scraps that haven't properly decomposed from the surface, extract your finished compost and add the scraps back.

Normally, compost should smell like the earth. If your compost doesn't have an earthly smell, that is an indication of a problem. The only exception to this if you are composting manure in your pile. That will generally make the pile stink until the manure breaks down.

However, if your compost is smelling without the presence of manure, the reasons could be any of the following:

• **Too Many Green Ingredients**: If you add too many food scraps and nitrogen ingredients into your pile, it will start smelling like ammonia or sewage. That is an indication that your carbon to nitrogen ratio is off balance. Adding more newspaper, straw, leaves, and other brown materials will help the heap regain balance.

• **Compaction**: A compacted compost heap is more likely to smell due to lack of aeration. If the materials are too close to one another, the pile will develop a putrid smell similar to rotting eggs. Frequently turning the pile will get air into it and stop the stink. You should also add more dry grass and dry leaves to stop the compost from compacting again.

• **High Moisture Level**: Compost tends to stink in spring due to frequent rains that make the compost wetter than needed. Moisture is important in composting, but it shouldn't be too much, or it'll block aeration. Adding brown materials and turning the pile should significantly reduce the moisture content. Also, if the rain remains unabated, cover your pile with a tarp or something similar to provide it with an extra layer of protection.

• **Layering:** Sometimes, gardeners get the right balance of brown and green materials, yet their piles stink. This often happens due to improper layering. If you don't layer your ingredients, the green waste will be isolated from the brown ones, leading to incorrect decomposition. That can cause the pile to start giving off a putrid smell. Mixing the pile a little better is the key to solving this problem.

Maintaining an odorless compost heap requires little effort. The basic step is to balance the brown and green ingredients in the pile, frequently turn the pile, and keep it moist. Keeping compost odorless starts with using only acceptable ingredients. As mentioned earlier, don't add meats and bones into your compost because they decompose slowly.

Organic waste, heat, water, and oxygen are the most important factors in composting. A careful balance of all four variables can help you achieve an odorless compost heap.

If one factor is out of place, the whole process is affected, and odor may arise. For example, suppose there isn't enough heat in a pile. In that case, the heat-loving organisms responsible for the breakdown of the organic materials won't initiate the second phase, leaving the materials sitting there and rotting, which results in unpleasant odors.

Follow these steps to manage stinky odors in your compost pile:

• Turn the pile at least once a week to add oxygen for the aerobic microbes that require it to decompose the waste.

• If you notice a strong ammonia smell, increase the carbon ingredients. Ammonia indicates excessive nitrogen levels.

• Keep the compost bin or pile in a location with full sun to keep it as warm as possible.

Odor management in compost is achievable as long as you maintain a balance of the four most important composting factors.

How to Know if Your Compost Pile Is Struggling

As explained, the right combination of water, heat, air, carbon, and nitrogen is the key to creating an environment for microbes to thrive in a pile. An imbalance of one or two of these will make your compost struggle to mature. So how do you know if a compost pile is struggling?

The first sign is when your pile is moist, yet your materials aren't breaking down. That means your pile isn't getting enough air to breathe. For optimal composting, you need the aerobic microbes to do their job, which can't happen if they don't get sufficient air/oxygen. So naturally, the solution to this is to turn your pile regularly or fluff it up with a pitchfork every couple of weeks.

As the previous heading explains, a compost pile should be odorless by default if you balance the vital components well. Therefore, an odorous compost indicates a struggling pile. Again, you can address that problem by turning the pile and adding more carbon materials. Repeat the process for as long as necessary until the smell is no longer there.

Sometimes, the carbon ingredients in a pile fail to break down, suggesting a problem – usually an imbalance carbon-to-nitrogen ratio. If your carbon ingredients aren't decomposing, add half as many nitrogen materials to the heap. Then, mix them in with a pitchfork and moisten thoroughly with water.

A common downside to having too many greens in your pile is the compost's susceptibility to combustion. Excessive nitrogen presence can make compost heat up too quickly, leading to a spontaneous fire outbreak. That automatically makes your compost a fire and health hazard.

As explained in a previous chapter, compost fires are rare and mostly happen in industrial composting areas. Still, it's important to pay attention to your heap and make sure it doesn't get too hot. The other problem is that hot compost can kill off your plants if you don't leave it to cool off for a short time.

A healthy compost contains a plethora of bugs, worms, mycelium, and mites. These organisms are usually visible during turning. If there are no worms or bugs in your compost, that means you are doing something wrong.

It takes a while for microbes to find new composts, especially when there is no other pile around. However, if you don't find any in your pile after a few weeks, you need to reexamine the C: N ratio and the moisture level.

Since you are probably starting your bin from scratch, you should add a few handfuls of existing composted material or manure to inoculate the new pile with beneficial organisms and attract even more microfauna.

The word "micro" in microorganisms tells us that the decomposing creatures in compost piles are tiny. That also tells us that they take tiny bites from organic materials. Adding large items such as sticks and twigs to the heap slows down decomposition considerably. Besides, those larger chunks of materials usually lack the moisture retention capacity needed to achieve an appropriate water balance. Always chop the materials into finer pieces to make decomposition easier on the living creatures in the pile.

As established at several points in the book, turning is the number one solution to most of the composting problems you are likely to face. Therefore, you should know that a turner is one of the most important tools to own before you get started on this composting journey.

Chapter Twelve: Growing Plants for a Compost Pile

Many gardeners are trying next-level composting, which involves growing plants specifically for compost instead of gathering materials from the kitchen and yard. This is something that you can try as you become more versed in the art of making organic compost.

Recycling your kitchen scraps and garden waste into rich, nutrient-filled humus for your soil and plants is great. But why stop there? You can progress even further by growing certain plants to make your black gold even richer than usual.

This method is a more intensive technique and isn't something you should try if you are a beginner. Basic composting is good for newbies. This method is for more experienced composters. Of course, you can give it a try, but we recommend giving it a shot after successfully making quality organic compost at least twice.

You grow specific plants and add them to your heap in specific ways. This practice is mostly used in bio-intensive gardening, but you can borrow from the previously covered composting techniques if you may not wish to embrace certain aspects of these gardening techniques.

There are various plants you can grow to improve the nutrient content of your organic compost. Most are easy to grow and incorporate into an outdoor garden. You can use them specifically for composting or other reasons.

One of the best choices is legumes – you can grow any kind of legume from alfalfa to clover. These plants contain healthy amounts of nitrogen and are easily grown between rows and edges of a garden. Harvest them and shred the clippings into your pile to boost the nitrogen content.

Some herbs are also excellent composting plants. Herbs like comfrey and borage grow quickly to produce lots of greens for the pile. In addition, they add essential nutrients such as zinc and phosphorus to compost. Comfrey also contains significant amounts of macronutrient potassium.

Comfrey

Another plant you can grow for composting is Yarrow – it boosts the process of decomposition. Next, add extra brassicas to your garden and add the excess to your compost pile. Examples of brassicas are Daikon Radish and Kale. Finally, use the other parts of the plants to enrich your compost with additional nutrients.

Yarrow

Growing plants for composting is a next-level way to enrich the quality of your soil and plants, plus it's effortless. If you have space and resources, you can start growing compost plants in different spots in your garden.

Conclusion

Congratulation, you have learned everything there is to know about the art of composting! Now it's time for you to get to work and start creating magic in your backyard. As established through the information in the book, organic composting is a relatively straightforward process. With the right guide, anyone can make organic compost in their home.

Each chapter in this book breaks down a different aspect of composting to help you achieve an in-depth understanding of the entire process. Most importantly, there are practical instructions and visual images to help you as you navigate through the book.

Nothing is stopping you from creating great compost!

Here's another book by Dion Rosser that you might like

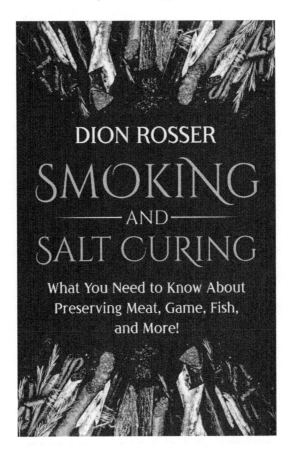

References

Backyard Composting Basics: A Cheatsheet. (2019, January 4). Rodale Institute. https://rodaleinstitute.org/blog/backyard-composting-basics-a-cheatsheet/

EarthEasy. (2019). Composting. Eartheasy Guides & Articles. https://learn.eartheasy.com/guides/composting/

US EPA, O. (2013, April 17). Composting At Home. US EPA. https://www.epa.gov/recycle/composting-home US EPA, OLEM. (2019, April 30). Types of Composting and Understanding the Process | US EPA. US EPA. https://www.epa.gov/sustainable-management-food/types-composting-and-understanding-process

Brennan, E. (2012, February 10). Gardening for beginners: Composting without a compost bin. Retrieved from Dengarden website: https://dengarden.com/gardening/How-to-Create-Luxurious-Garden-Compost

Burgard, D. (2018, July 31). Critters in your compost? - FineGardening. Retrieved from Finegardening.com website: https://www.finegardening.com/article/critters-in-your-compost

Carroll, J. (2014, September 8). Vermicomposting worm types - what are the best worms for compost bin. Retrieved from Gardeningknowhow.com website: https://www.gardeningknowhow.com/composting/vermicomposting/worms-for-vermicomposting.htm

Carry on composting ~ Compost activators, accelerators, inoculators and makers. (n.d.). Retrieved from Carryoncomposting.com website: http://www.carryoncomposting.com/443725785

Compost in Your Garden: Why You Need it & How to do it Right. (2020, May 16). Retrieved from Growmyownfood.com website: https://growmyownfood.com/compost-in-garden/

Engels, J. (2020, August 14). How to compost without a compost bin - one green planet. Retrieved from Onegreenplanet.org website: https://www.onegreenplanet.org/lifestyle/compost-without-a-bin/

FINISHED COMPOST. (n.d.). HOW TO USE COMPOST. Retrieved from Earthmatter.org website: https://earthmatter.org/wp-content/uploads/2016/08/tip-sheet-how-to-use-compost-cpts-htuc-f.pdf

Green, C. (2021, May 5). How to start a traditional compost pile in your yard. Retrieved from Chelseagreen.com website: https://www.chelseagreen.com/2020/how-to-start-a-traditional-compost-pile-in-your-yard/

How to build a compost pile. (2014, March 16). Retrieved from Planetnatural.com website: https://www.planetnatural.com/composting-101/making/compost-pile/

How to compost without a bin. (n.d.). Retrieved from Rootsnursery.com website: https://rootsnursery.com/how-to-compost-without-a-bin/

Hu, S. (n.d.). Composting 101. Retrieved from Nrdc.org website: https://www.nrdc.org/stories/composting-101

Hunt, K. (2018, December 7). What is composting? Retrieved from Greenmatters.com website:

https://www.greenmatters.com/food/2018/12/07/ZboPlt/what-is-composting

Managing bugs in your compost - the good, the bad, and the merely ugly. (n.d.). Retrieved from Davesgarden.com website: https://davesgarden.com/guides/articles/view/3942

No title. (n.d.). Retrieved from Happycow.net website: https://www.happycow.net/blog/container-composting/

Ross, R. (2018, September 12). The science behind composting. Retrieved from Livescience.com website: https://www.livescience.com/63559-composting.html

State of California. (n.d.). Vermicomposting: Composting with Worms. Retrieved from Calrecycle.ca.gov website: https://www.calrecycle.ca.gov/organics/worms/wormfact

Tilley, N. (2014, May 10). Instructions for composting - how to start compost for gardens. Retrieved from Gardeningknowhow.com website: https://www.gardeningknowhow.com/composting/basics/starting-compost-pile.htm

Tools You Need for Composting - dummies. (2016, March 26). Retrieved from Dummies.com website: https://www.dummies.com/home-garden/green-living/tools-you-need-for-composting/

Ullman, M., & Burke, O. (2021, April 23). The 4 best compost bins to help fertilize your garden in 2021. *Business Insider*. Retrieved from https://www.businessinsider.com/best-compost-bin

Using your compost. (n.d.). Retrieved from Recyclenow.com website: https://www.recyclenow.com/reduce-waste/composting/using-your-compost

Vermicomposting - Composting with Worms. (n.d.). Retrieved from Ucanr.edu website: https://ucanr.edu/blogs/blogcore/postdetail.cfm?postnum=17055

(N.d.-a). Retrieved from Commongroundcompost.com website: http://commongroundcompost.com/what-is-compost/learning-to-compost/tools-for-composting/

(N.d.-b). Retrieved from Compostjunkie.com

Printed in Great Britain
by Amazon